The Modern-Day Pharisees: "The Uncovering"

Thirty-Four Years in Ministry
What You Can Learn From My Experience

By
Dr. Jake Williams Jr

The Modern-Day Pharisees: "The Uncovering"
Thirty-Four Years in Ministry
What You Can Learn From My Experience
Copyright © 2025
Dr. Jake Williams Jr

ALL RIGHTS RESERVED.
No part of this publication may be reproduced, stored in any electronic system, or transmitted in any form or by any means, electronic, mechanical, photocopy, recording, or otherwise, without express written permission from the author.

Cover Art:
La' Won D. Williams
and
Dr. Jake Williams Jr
Editing by:
Dr. Barbara W. Williams

Unless otherwise indicated, all Scripture quotations are taken from the King James Version of the Bible.

ISBN: 978-0-9986590-1-5
First printing: December 2025

FOR MORE BOOKS OR INFORMATION CONTACT:
Dr. Jake Williams Jr, Pastor
Jesus World Outreach Center, Inc.
PO Box 41424
Fayetteville, NC 28309
(910) 823-4849

Please visit our website at:
www.jwocnc.org

DEDICATION:

I want to dedicate this book to my church members that have remained faithful to the vision. Who have believed in my wife and me to be God sent and have allowed us to pastor them by feeding them with knowledge and understanding of God's Word. Thank you for your love and support.

ACKNOWLEDGEMENTS:

God the Father, His Son **Jesus** and the **Holy Spirit** for guiding me and reminding me to always be steadfast and unmovable.

My wife, Barbara, and our children for their love, support and patience.

My parents, Jake and Ruthie Mae Williams, for giving me life and love, by training me in the way that I should go.

Table of Contents

DEDICATION: 3
ACKNOWLEDGEMENTS: 4
INTRODUCTION: 6
Chapter 1: The Modern-Day Pharisee 9
Chapter 2: My Decision To Stand 28
Chapter 3: My Dirt: Here Is My Wrongness 35
Chapter 4: The Vision Began 45
Chapter 5: Grand Opening Service 64
Chapter 6: Everyone Has Some Wrongness 78
Chapter 7: The Narcissistic Leader 125
Chapter 8: Our Covenant 133
Chapter 9: Leaders That Answers To No One 192
Chapter 10: Be A Better You 214
Chapter 11: Beware Of Man Pleasers 246
Other books published by this author: 272
"Breaking Traditions" 272

INTRODUCTION:

The Modern-Day Pharisees: The Uncovering. Thirty-Four Years in Ministry, What You Can Learn From My Experience.

To the readers of this book, I believe by the leading and the guiding of the Holy Spirit, I have been inspired to write this book. This book is NOT written in chronological order, so I encourage you to read the entire book before trying to judge the contents of it. **Proverbs 18:13** says, *"He that answereth a matter before he heareth it, it is foolish, and shame unto him."* So first hear the conclusion of the whole matter, before trying to judge this book. I believe through this information, and the things that I will expose in this book, will help those that are in leadership position or future leaders to be better leaders. The Modern-Day Pharisees: The Uncovering, is all about the uncovering of hidden sins, the exposing of wrongness in leadership today. I will talk about, and discuss the narcissistic leader, which is a person who has an excessive interest in or admiration of themselves, one's physical appearance, selfish, vanity, a lack of empathy, and are very controlling. The narcissistic leader is in it solely for his or her own enrichment, it's all about themselves, and that is The Modern-Day Pharisees: The Uncovering, which I will be discussing throughout this book. You will learn from my mistakes as well as others that has made mistakes, that we are not the only ones, and there will be others, but you don't have to make the same mistakes that we made. The only reason why I will expose and talk about the people and the things that I have experienced in ministry in this book, is to help you future leaders to be better leaders. This book is not what you are probably thinking of when it comes to The Modern-Day Pharisees: The Uncovering. It is not a book about spiritual insight or law versus grace or doctrine. It's a book about my real-life experienced of being in ministry for thirty-four years, and being able to identify and expose this present-day Pharisee. I call them, The Modern-Day Pharisees, and it's all about the uncovering of their hidden sins, and how they hide in plain sight, and do their deals in secret, under cover. I will talk about, and discuss my experience of the leadership in three different churches that I was a member, and a leader in, while serving in the military. It is my intentions to expose what has been going on for years in the church and are still going on today, but undercover. There are very few that will stand-up for what is right and will speak out against it, because of fear of retribution, from church leaders. It's amazing how church leaders can claim to be so righteous, and holy, but yet be so deep in hidden sin, and far from being obedient to what God has called them to do. This is the life of the modern-day Pharisees to hide with they are doing but expose others. This book is about how the modern-day Pharisees operate in plain sight working their deals, being man pleases to each other and doing their deals and stealing from the church. My intent of writing this book, is to identify and to expose what some religious leaders has been doing, and some still doing, and in some cases illegal, and they are doing it in the name of the Lord. This book is about the uncovering of the modern-day Pharisee, what they do in secret, and what you can learn from my experience of being in ministry for thirty-four years. Based on my eyewitness account of these things that has been going on by leaders in the church, I have written them just as I have seen, heard, and experienced them, but they are not in chronological order. In **Matthew the 23rd chapter** Jesus called the scribes and Pharisees, *fools and blind, hypocrites*! Jesus chastised them because of their self-righteous attitude, and the way they lived and how they judged and treated others.

At the conclusion of this book, I believe that the information that has been presented throughout this book, will have revealed, and uncovered, the modern-day Pharisee in this day and time. I believe you will be able to identify the modern-day Pharisee, that are operating in the churches today.

Chapter 1: The Modern-Day Pharisee

This book is about my thirty-four years in ministry, what you can learn from my experience. This book was not written out of anger or to put anyone down but to expose what has been and is still going on in churches today as I have seen it. This book is NOT written in chronological order, so I encourage you to read the entire book before trying to judge the contents of it. **Proverbs 18:13** says, *"He that answereth a matter before he heareth it, it is foolish, and shame unto him."* So first hear the conclusion of the whole matter, before trying to judge this book. To the readers of this book, I believe by the leading and the guidance of the Holy Spirit, I have been inspired to write this book. It is my intentions to present information to you that will help you in your leadership walk with others. I believe through this information, and the things that I will expose in this book, will help those that are in leadership position or future leaders to be better leaders. The Modern-Day Pharisees: The Uncovering, is all about the uncovering of hidden sins, the exposing of wrongness in leadership today. You will learn from my mistakes as well as others that has made mistakes, that we are not the only ones, and there will be others, but you don't have to make the same mistakes that we made. The only reason why I will expose and talk about myself, and others, and the things that I have experienced in ministry in this book, is to be transparent. This book is not what you are probably thinking of when it comes to The Modern-Day Pharisees: The

Uncovering. It is not a book about spiritual insight or law versus grace, or doctrine. It's a book about my real-life experienced of being in ministry for thirty-four years, and being able to identify and expose this present-day Pharisees. I call them, The Modern-Day Pharisees: The Uncovering, and how they hide in plain sight, and do their deals under cover. I will talk about, and discuss my experience of the leadership in three different churches that I was a member, and a leader in, while serving in the military. It is not my intention to put anyone on blast, or to expose anyone by calling their name, or the name of their church, or to get back at anyone. It is to expose what has been going on for years in the church and are still going on today, but undercover, and you need to be able to identify it. There are very few that will stand-up for what is right and will speak out against it, because of fear of retribution from church leaders. Anyone that knows me might know some of those that I am referring to in this book, but it just might not be the person that you are thinking of, because it might be you. You've heard that old saying "if the shoe fit, wear it". In other words if you are doing these things, or have been doing these things, or some of these things, then yes, I'm talking about you. There is more than one person in the world that has done the same as someone else. So, you might think you know who I'm referring to, but maybe it's not that person at all. It's amazing how church leaders can claim to be so righteous, and holy, but yet be so deep in hidden sin, and far from being obedient to what God has called them to do. This is the life of the modern-day Pharisees to hide with they are doing but expose others. This book is about how the modern-day Pharisees operate in plain sight working their deals, being man pleases to each other and doing their deals and stealing from the church. My intent of writing this book, is to identify and to expose what some religious leaders has been doing, and some still doing, and in some cases illegal, and they are doing it in the name of the Lord. This book is more about the uncovering of the modern-day Pharisee, and what you can learn from my experience of being in ministry for thirty-four years. It is to help the next generation of pastors, and church leaders that they don't fall into the same traps, and pitfalls as others by continuing the cycle, but to help break it. They can learn from other people's mistakes and other people's examples. I talk about, the good, and the bad, that I've seen, heard and experienced in ministry, and I pray that you can learn and draw from these things that you don't repeat the cycle. This book tells, and show how the modern-day Pharisee operate in this day and time. How they forced their will upon others, to force them to do what they want them to do. How they do their deals and secret, behind closed doors, from the public eyes. How they abuse, their authority and their positions, because they have no one to answer to. How they, self-promote themselves, and how they pretend to be something that they're not. How they are man pleasers, and people pleasers with certain ones in the ministry to help hide what they're doing. These things that I am talking about in this book are true, and a lot of these things that I'm referring to in this book, I have backed them up with audio recordings as proof, and notes **for myself**. Remember, these are the things that I have seen, heard, and experienced in real life for thirty-four years in ministry. Based on my eyewitness account of these things that has been going on by leaders in the church, I have written them just as I have seen, heard, and experienced them, but they are not in chronological order. These are things that leaders have been, and are still doing and they trying to hide their activities from others. It is my intent to expose these types of leaders in this book so that others might be able to identify and know them for themselves.

We know what the Pharisee looked and acted like in Jesus' time, but what does the modern-day Pharisee look like, and act like today? They look and ack like you and me, but they have a hidden agenda. In this book, you will be able to identify the modern-day Pharisee, and their hidden agenda, and how they work their deals. They are all about themselves, they're all about being seen, they are all about having their way. The modern-day Pharisee does not repent from sin, or wrongdoing, because they believe that they have no sin or have done no wrong. They believe and think that God actually need them, and God can only use them, and no one else. When talking with them they will always dominate the conversation, it will always be a monologue with them and never a dialogue, because they want to control which direction the conversation goes. They want to make sure that nothing is said by others to reveal their actions, that's why they will dominate the conversation to make sure that that doesn't happen. They are quick to lie on others, and embellish the story and make it more than what it is. They will hide in their ministry, in their own little corner of the world, and isolate their people from others, telling them not to listen to other preachers, or people. They will tell their people whatever THEY want them to believe, and their people will believe it because you are their pastor, but not understanding, just because you said it, or told it to them, doesn't make it the truth. They are quick to defend themselves by deflecting, and shifting the blame to others to get the attention off of themselves. They are quick to get people around themselves that would go along to get along. They are always looking for someone that will agree with them and their actions, even when they are wrong. They know what to say to others to get them to do something, but will never do it themselves. They preach, but they do not practice what they preach. They are one way in front of people in public, but a different way behind closed doors out of the public's sight. They are pretenders, they pretend that their ministries are all that, and all that they do are successful, when really it is not, it's just a front to make it look like it's something that it's not. They lack empathy, and compassion for others, and don't know how to walk in true love. They will self-promote themselves, because they are not under anyone's authority, so they answer to no one. They will see greatness in others, but will put them down, because it's all about themselves. They are not givers, they give very little, but expect much in return from others, and their church. These are the characteristics of the modern-day Pharisee, whom I shall be talking about throughout this book. I encourage you as you read this book, look for these characteristics, and you will spot the modern-day Pharisee that is operating in this day and time. At the conclusion of this book, I believe that the information that has been presented throughout this book, will have revealed, and uncovered, the modern-day Pharisees operating in the churches today.

Let's dive into what God has revealed and has instructed me to write. We are starting to see a lot of great men and women who were once great in the body of Christ begin to fall, through God's uncovering, and it's on public display. I hate to see it on public display because the first thing the world does is point there finger back at the church. But maybe we need to have someone's fingers pointed back at us, because judgment must first begin with us. I believe there is a reason why some of these great men and women of God, were put on public display, and some has even died a premature death. I believe God gives every leader the opportunity to uncover their own sins, by confessing, and owning them, but when they refuse to do so, God Himself will uncover you and expose your sin for all to see. There was a well-known pastor of a megachurch some years ago, that went to prison for defrauding his members out of millions of dollars. While in prison, he was interviewed by a reporter, and were asked the question, when did you go wrong? He replied I went wrong when I lost the fear of God, and that was my downfall. I believe in this day and time, a lot of religious leaders has lost the fear of God, **not as in respect, or honor**, <u>but a fear of</u>

<u>what could happen to them at the Judgment Seat of Christ</u>. **2 Corinthians 5:10** says, *"For we must all appear before the judgment seat of Christ; that everyone may receive the things done in his body, according to that he hath done, whether it be good or bad."* **Ecclesiastes 12:14** says, *"For God shall bring every work into judgment, with every secret thing, whether it be good, or whether it be evil."* You can see in these two scriptures nothing shall be hidden everything shall be revealed. You will give an account whether it be good, bad, or evil, but you will give an account for your actions or a lack of action there of. I believe God gives every person the space to repent, but your pride won't let you. You have every opportunity to repent, and make things right against those you have wronged, but you refuse to do so, because you have lost the fear of God. **Hebrews 10:30-31** says, *"...<u>The Lord shall judge his people</u>. **It is a fearful thing to fall into the hands of the living God.**"* This word **<u>fearful</u>** truly means, you as a leader should be afraid of what awaits you at the judgment seat of Christ because of what you have been doing, or not doing as a leader. Some religious leaders stand in the pull-pit living their lives one way in the church, but outside of the church they live a totally different lifestyle. Those that has had a public fall from Grace, I honestly believe that before their public fall, the Holy Spirit was trying His best to catch them in their prayer time, but they just wouldn't listen. They always saw themselves right and everyone else wrong, they were so full of themselves, and of their self-righteous attitude. This is exactly how the modern-day Pharisee think

and act in this day and time. They do their deals and secret, undercover, hidden from the public eyes, but the all-seeing eye of God sees them, and great were, or shall be their fall. God could not allow them to continue in ministry or to represent Him, because it would send the wrong message to them, and that's why there were a public uncovering of their sins.

Let's define the word **Pharisee,** it means, *"a sanctimonious (self-righteous), or hypocritical show of religion devotion; a person, that pretends to have qualities, beliefs, or feelings that they do not really have."*

Let's look at the book of Matthew, the 23rd chapter, and see the Pharisees in Jesus' time, and how He chastised them because of their self-righteous attitude, and the way they lived and how they judged and treated others.

Matthew 23:13-29,33 *"But woe unto you, scribes and Pharisees, hypocrites! for ye shut up the kingdom of heaven against men: for ye neither go in yourselves, neither suffer ye them that are entering to go in. Woe unto you, scribes and Pharisees, hypocrites! for ye devour widows' houses, and for a pretense make long prayer: therefore, ye shall receive the greater damnation. Woe unto you, scribes and Pharisees, hypocrites! for ye compass sea and land to make one proselyte, and when he is made, ye make him twofold more the child of hell than yourselves. Woe unto you, ye blind guides, which say, Whosoever shall swear by* *the temple, it is nothing; but whosoever shall swear by the gold of the temple, he is a debtor! Ye fools and blind: for whether is greater, the gold, or the temple that sanctifieth the gold? And, Whosoever shall swear by the altar, it is nothing; but whosoever sweareth by the gift that is upon it, he is guilty. Ye fools and blind: for whether is greater, the gift, or the altar that sanctifieth the gift? Whoso therefore shall swear by the altar, sweareth by it, and by all things thereon. And whoso shall swear by the temple, sweareth by it, and by him that dwelleth therein. And he that shall swear by heaven, sweareth by the throne of God, and by him that sitteth thereon. Woe unto you, scribes and Pharisees, hypocrites! for ye pay tithe of mint and anise and cummin, and have omitted the weightier matters of the law, judgment, mercy, and faith: these ought ye to have done, and not to leave the other undone. Ye blind guides, which strain at a gnat, and swallow a camel. Woe unto you, scribes and Pharisees, hypocrites! for ye make clean the outside of the cup and of the platter, but within they are full of extortion and excess. Thou blind Pharisee, cleanse first that which is within the cup and platter, that the outside of them may be clean also. Woe unto you, scribes and Pharisees, hypocrites! for ye are like unto whited sepulchres* (graves), *which indeed appear beautiful outward, but are within full of dead men's bones, and of all uncleanness. Even so ye also outwardly appear righteous unto men, but within ye are full of hypocrisy and iniquity. Woe unto you, scribes and Pharisees, hypocrites! because ye build the tombs of the prophets, and garnish the sepulchres* (graves) *of the righteous. Ye serpents, ye generation of vipers, how can ye escape the damnation of hell?"*

Jesus called them, *fools and blind, hypocrites*! Notice, seven times He called those *scribes and Pharisees* hypocrites. Then He identified what they were doing that made them hypocrites. He said you are like *"a grave, which indeed appear beautiful outward, but inward full of deadman bones and full of all uncleanness."* Not some uncleanness, but all uncleanness. He went on to say, *"outwardly, you appear onto man as though you're righteous but, inward you are full of hypocrisy and iniquity."* Now look at what it says in Luke chapter 12, and what Jesus have to say about hypocrisy, and the warning He gives to his disciples. In **Luke 12:1-3** it says, *"...he began to say unto his disciples **first of all**, **Beware ye of the leaven of the Pharisees, which is hypocrisy**. For there is nothing covered, that shall not be revealed; neither hid, that shall not be known. Therefore whatsoever ye have spoken in darkness shall be heard in the light; and that which ye have spoken in the ear in closets shall be proclaimed upon the housetops."* If you go back and read all three versus you will see that there was a large crowd, thousands of people there pressing in, waiting to hear Jesus speak. But can you imagine, the first words out of His mouth was not about miracles, not about blessings, not about healing, but a warning to his disciples; **"beware of the leaven of the Pharisees, which is hypocrisy**." Let's look at the word **hypocrisy,** and what it actually means.

Hypocrisy, which is being a ***hypocrite***, which mean; *"an actor; you act one way in public, but behind closed doors you are completely different; you are a person that pretends to have qualities, beliefs, or feelings that you do not really have; it's your character, it's who we really are."* Notice, the definition of a hypocrites has the same characteristics and definition of a Pharisee, ***which is a pretender***. Based on this definition, I believe Jesus is saying, you are not real, you are an actor, you are a pretender, and there is nothing good that can come from you. Jesus went on to say, in Luke chapter 12 about the Pharisees, hiding what they do, but in public pretend to be so holy, and that's what makes them a hypocrite. Jesus is warning us, that every secret thing you have done, good or bad will come out. He's letting us know, you can fool people, but you can't fool God, and those things that you have spoken or done in secret shall be revealed openly. Jesus is warning His disciples and us, don't be a hypocrite, don't be like them, be careful what you say and do in secret. At the end of this chastisement in Matthew chapter 23, Jesus called the Pharisees serpents, generation of vipers, snakes. He told them how they can't escape the damnation to come. I don't care who you are, or what title you may have, if you are walking in the footsteps of the Pharisees that Jesus is referring to in these scripture, there will be a day of reckoning. In this modern day and time, you will not be able to escape the punishment or damnation to come. I believe Jesus is telling you to turn ye, turn ye, you wicked leaders, from your wicked ways, before it's too late.

This is how the Pharisees operated in Jesus' time, as well as this day and time. They do what they do in the name of God to appear spiritual, and they say I'm pushing fourth, and advancing the Kingdom for God. These things have the Lord allowed me to have seen, heard and experienced for thirty-four years in ministry at the time when He told me to write this book. He said to me "write these things down and keep them in your heart, for these are the modern-day Pharisee, which hide in plain sight, and conduct their business and work their deals day by day in My name." So, I started making notes, writing down and in some cases even recording what I heard and what I saw. These things that I am writing in this book are true, and it is what you can learn from my experience in ministry.

Let me tell you a little bit about myself. I am from the country and grew up in a small-town call Seale, Alabama. We were sharecroppers working the land, and also textile mill workers. I was brought up in the Baptist church, and at age fourteen I join the local church, got water baptized, song in the junior choir, was a junior usher, and thought that I was saved because I had done these things. **Titus 3:5** says, *"not by works of righteousness which we have done, but according to his mercy he saved us, by the washing of regeneration, and renewing of the Holy Ghost."* In May 1975 at age seventeen, I graduated high school, but I was not college material, so for the next year I worked a dead-end job in the textile mill leading me to nowhere. I never will forget one day my dad called me into the room and said sit down son let me talk to you. He said two years ago your oldest brother graduated high school immediately went into the Air Force. He said now your younger brother is getting ready to graduate high school and has already signed up to go into the U.S. Army. He said to me, for one year I have let you sit around here to make your own decisions for your life, but it seems to me you're not going to make one. He said, so, I'm going to make one for you. "Either you're going to college are you going into the military, but you are going to get out of here *(my house),* by me allowing you to stay here is not helping you in life." That was one of the best things that my dad could ever say to me. It forced me to make a decision to do something meaningful with my life. The adventure began in August 1976 at age eighteen, I joined the U.S. Army, where I serve faithfully for twenty-two years, retiring in September 1998, at the rank of Sergeant First Class (SFC/E-7). I went to college and earned my doctorate degree in Christian Education/Counseling. Later in May 2006, I went to flight school, and became a commercial pilot, join the Civil Air Patrol, serving as a Mission Search and Rescue Pilot. Leaving home and joining the military, was one of the best things that I could have ever done, it changed my life forever. That decision set me on a path and a course that God had prepared for me, and I had no idea how it would affect my life.

While serving in the military in 1988 I got station overseas, and while there, I was playing semi-pro professional baseball, living the club life, and living like the world. I believe, I was just going to church on Sunday morning just to soothe my conscious. I really wasn't serving God because my nature hadn't changed. I was doing things the way I learned in the traditional church, lived the way you want to live six days a week and go to church on Sunday and everything will be all right. That's the biggest con Satan ever came up with and I had fallen for it hook, line and sinker the fisherman, his reel and rod and his boots. He had me hooked bad. One day my younger brother and his wife got stationed in the same place I was stationed at. They invited me to go to this little non-denominational church with them where this preacher was teaching the Word not preaching. Preaching is what I was used to in the Baptist church, but he was teaching the Word with simplicity and understanding. After putting my brother off several times of inviting me, I finally capitulated and went. To hear the Word of God taught the way it was being taught open my spiritual eyes and it changed my life forever. I received Jesus Christ as my Savior and Lord in October 1989 at age thirty-two while tending this church. For the next year I grew in wisdom and knowledge in the things of God because faith came to me by hearing the Word of God. To make a long story short, the military sent me back to the states to be stationed at Fort Gordon Georgia but before I left, my pastor spoke a word into my life, and that word was, God has a call on your life and He will make it known to you in it's time, just wait on the Lord. My pastor told me satan will come to test me, to get me off the course that God has already prepared for me. He told me, I don't know what kind of test, but I will be tested, to see will I be found faithful to what it's truth and what is right.

The Test:

In 1991 while station at Fort Gordon Georgia, the test came. I was attending bible study in the afternoons with the soldiers, where the unit chaplain taught the class. I can say this man truly had a call on his life from God. It wasn't just a job to him it was truly a calling. After about six months of attending the bible study classes, the chaplain informed me that he would be leaving being reassigned to Korea. He asked me would I take over the bible study classes until the new chaplain arrive. I told him I didn't think I was ready to step into his shoes, teaching the class, but he assured me that I was ready he said just trust God. He got permission from the Battalion Commander *(Lieutenant Colonel)*, that I would take over the bible study classes in the afternoon with the soldiers and that I have his permission to continue teaching the class until the new replacement chaplain arrived. I took over the bible study when the chaplain left, but I was ridiculed by others that was not in the class, saying that as a non-commission officer (NCO), and a drill sergeant, I shouldn't be teaching the bible study classes to the soldiers, because I am not a chaplain. They said, we should wait until the new chaplain arrive; **they gave me hell**. In the unit I saw a lot of wrongness going on, a lot of shady deals being made, by NCO's, and offices that had no integrity. They were being men pleases to each other, in the military it's called <u>butt kissing</u>, so that you can get promoted, move up or be put into certain positions. The younger soldiers of less rank were being mistreated verbally and physically, and no one was doing anything about it. As a christian or non-christian everyone could see what was going on was wrong, but no one did anything. The test was, would I do anything about it, or would I just go along to get along? As a Sergeant First Class/E7 or above, you move into the political ram of things in the military. It was no longer about how well you knew your job or could do your job, but it was more about pleasing your boss or whose butt you were going to kiss. They expect you to be a team player in spite of. They expect you to go along to get along. They expect you to see it and not see it, to hear it and not hear it, do it, and not question it, and that's what most people did to protect their own careers and to get promoted. But not me! My **integrity** compelled me to do what is right. My integrity compelled me to stand for what I know to be right **even at great personal cost**. And that's the problem that I see in most churches, and in most organizations, people will see wrongness, but will not speak up, or stand for what is right. They will see it, but will say or do nothing just to protect their own careers. God has to have a channel that he can work through. God is not going to speak out of the sky to correct the wrongness, He has to have someone that has integrity, and is willing to stand, that He can work through. As leaders, your integrity MUST always compel you to stand for what is right, **even at great personal costs**.

Side Note, **Integrity:**

    Proverbs 11:3 says, *"The integrity of the*

24

upright shall guide them... ." Our integrity should always guide us, what does that mean? Integrity helps us to see the truth and what is right and what is wrong, and we choose to do what is right. It's a choice. Integrity always has a price tag attached to it. What do I mean? When it comes to integrity, either you will pay a smaller price in the beginning for being a person of integrity or you will pay a greater price at the end for not being a person of integrity. But you will pay a price, which price will you pay? There are three principles or components to integrity:

1. Discerning what is right and what is wrong. What does that mean? The word discern means to **know** to **see** to **understand**. So, this is telling me that I must **know, see** and **understand** what is right and what is wrong. One may look and say well that's easy, everyone knows the different between right and wrong. Not so, just look at the action or a lack of action in the lives of a lot of people when it comes to right or wrong.

2. Acting on what you have discern to be right even at great personal cost. Pastors and leaders, this is the part we don't want to do. Acting requires action of you. It requires you to do something and or say something even if it cost you, your promotion, your position or favor or friendship with others. As a christian, you must be willing to pay **great personal cost**

and stand against wrongness just as Jesus did. The word christian means Christlike, so that means we should follow His example and stand against wrongness no matter what the cost is.

3. Saying openly that I am acting on my understanding of right and wrong. That means, you can't be covert with your conversation, not hidden or not behind closed doors, but in your conversation and your actions they are right out in front of everyone, so they know where you stand on that matter.

Listen to me leaders as you read this. Where there is no possibility of lost, integrity cannot exist. What do I mean? It simply means, you don't know if you are a person of integrity until you have been tested or challenged with the possibility of losing something, and then you do what it takes to keep it without compromising what is right or what is truth. If you have never been challenged ***in an area***, you will never know what you'll really do. Integrity is the basis *(foundation)* of trust. Can I trust you, Can I be trusted, can God trust us? **Trust must be earned.** Pastors your character must say to your leaders, and congregation, at all times, I can be trusted. When you lie, or treat people wrong, you have broken trust, and **you now have to earn the right to be trusted again**, and that takes work, and time. God can't afford to trust us if we can't be trusted.
Consistency and **Predictability** are crucial to

integrity. Consistency means, you can count on me, to always to be at church or bible study no matter what. You are predictable to do the same things that you've been doing, and doing them in a timely matter, no matter what. You and your word are one. If your word is no good, that means you're no good. You are only as good as your word. Can people count on you? **Proverbs 25:19** says, *"Confidence in an unfaithful man in time of trouble is like a broken tooth, and a foot out of joint."* If you ever have to depend on, or put your trust in someone who lack integrity, who is undependable, unfaithful, untrustworthy, or uncommitted, is very painful. It's truly like a broken tooth or a foot out of joint. I should know, I have physically had a broken tooth, and I have physically had a broken ankle, and it's very painful. Having to have to depend on these types of people is very painful, because you have no confidence in them. Is your word any good? Can people count on your word? God is only as good as His Word, and God has placed His word above His name. **Psalms 138:2** says, *"...for thou hast magnified thy word above all thy name."* God gives more attention to His Word than even his name. Will you pay the price to be a person of integrity, and keep your word no matter what? What price will you pay? Will you pay great personal cost? Remember the person of integrity will take a stand on the principles of what they have discerned to be right **even at great personal cost**.

Chapter 2: My Decision To Stand

Back to what I was saying in chapter one, before I ventured off on this side note on integrity. I know this book is more about the modern-day Pharisees, the uncovering of them, and how they conduct themselves in the church, but I want you to understand, and know they're in **EVERY** organization, and not just in the church only. The test for me was, would I do anything about the wrongness that was going on, or would I just go along to get along, see it, and not see it, hear it, and not hear it, do it and not question it? If we all keep silent doing injustice, then where is justice? Keeping silent or doing nothing when you see wrongness is **NOT** integrity, because that is known as a **LACK** of integrity. We must be people of integrity and take a stand against this type of authority, no matter who or where it is. So I would like to show you in this chapter, how I took a stand while serving in the military, against this type of leadership authority from the modern-day Pharisee, **and I did it at the possibility of GREAT personal cost to my seventeen year military career**. God is always looking for someone that has integrity, and is full of faith, that is willing to stand for what is right, that he can work through. Remember the modern-day Pharisee is all about themselves, and no one else. It's all about them, having their way, abusing their authority, hiding, and covering what they do. They are all about having absolute power, and lording that power over others, no matter who it hurt or offend. True power doesn't come from your status, it comes from your character, because CHARACTER IS WHO WE REALLY ARE. True power isn't about making others feel small by lording that power over them, or getting back at them, or getting revenge. It's about using that power to lift others up, and using it to take a stand against wrongness, and to change the system from within.

Case in point. While serving in the military in 1991, and being station at Fort Gordon, in Augusta Georgia, my big test came. I held my peace as long as I could, and decided enough is enough! I went to the S3 captain and became a **whistleblower, and reported everything that I had observed and heard for months.** She said to me I'm willing to write the report and make a formal complaint but be warned, they are not going to like this, it's going to make the unit look bad. They're going to come after you with vengeance, I know you haven't done anything wrong but they're going to fabricate things on you. They're going to drag your name through the mud, and they are going to come up with bogus and false charges so they can Court-Martial you to get rid of you and say you were the problem, and sweep the real problem under the rug. Now you have heard what they're going to do, what do you want to do? She said before you answer I want to let you know I'm getting out of the military because I can't do this anymore. I can't keep going along to get along any longer. I will be out the military in three months, and you will be on your own. What do you want to do? I said, **"report it."** I will stand for what is right even at great personal cost.

Two weeks after the unit chaplain left and was reassigned to Korea. They brought me in and read me my rights. You know, *"you have the right to remain silent, anything you say can, and will be used against you in a court of law..."* and so on. I said what is going on, what did I do? They said, you were given a lawful order by the Battalion Commander not to teach bible study. You disobeyed that lawful order by continuing to teach. I said that's not true, the Chaplin, before he left, had gotten permission from the Battalion Commander, authorizing me to teach until the new replacement chaplain arrived. You can imagine the Battalion Commander did not back me up on that. He pretended that he had no idea what I was talking about. But that's OK, God always has a ram in the bush. Meaning, it's all part of God's plan. So, they brought me up on bogus and false charges, and swept the real problem under the rug just as the S3 captain said. I now know how Jesus felt, when the Pharisees and the Sadducees brought him up on trumped-up charges, and there was no one to back him up.

I was charged with:
    1. Failure to obey a general regulation or order.
    2. Disobeying a lawful order.
    3. Failure to perform your duties.
    4. Article 92 *(Article 92 defines disobeying a direct order as three types of offenses - violations or failures to obey lawful general orders or regulations, failures to obey other lawful orders, and dereliction of duty. Article 92 charges are*

common in many prosecutions. It does not take very much effort for the government to find an allegation under Article 92 in most cases, it's a catch all).

5. Conduct unbecoming of an NCO.

6. Indecent exposure.

7. Preaching without a license, and embezzling.

Later, the embezzling charge was dropped, because there was no money involved. They couldn't get anyone to say that attendant the bible studies that I was taking up money. Anyone that knows me or have known me, could easily tell that these bogus and false charges is not my character. You can tell by these charges, that they were really out to get me. **But I stood my ground, even at great personal cost**. **Ephesians 6:13** says, *"Wherefore take unto you the whole amour of God, that ye may be able to withstand in the evil day, and having done all, to stand."* When you have done all that you know to do, now stand! God will fight the battle for you, because the battle is not yours, it's the Lord's! Pastors, someday in our spiritual walk, we all are going to have to face the giant that is right in front of us just as David did with Goliath, and just as I did. That giant will look like a no win situation, and the deck is stacked against you, but what will you do? The devil will always make the problem or the battle look bigger than it really is, just as he did with David. Will you stand and be a person of faith and integrity, and let God use you, or will you operate in fear, and not stand? I encourage you to stand up for what is right even a great personal cost, and not be moved by what you see, and let the Lord fight the battle for you, because he has to have someone he can speak and work through, because the wrong has to be made right.

An article 32 hearing was held to see if there was enough evidence to go to trial. The prosecuting attorney said that there was not enough evidence to go to trial, everything that is listed here, its only hearsay, but he left it up to the unit Commander and the Command Sergeant Major. The Commander left the decision to the Command Sergeant Major, and the Command Sergeant Major told them, **go to trial**. He *(meaning me)* might slip up and say something that he didn't mean to say that we can get him on, and besides this, the chaplain has already left for Korea. Little did they know my attorney was bringing the chaplain back from Korea to testify on my behalf. Even though the Battalion Commander had amnesia in memory, the chaplain didn't. To make a long story short, after about four months, we went to trial. The chaplain testified on my behalf. It was an all-day trial that started at 0830 hours *(that's 8:30am)* and ended at all about 2030 hours *(that's 8:30pm)*. After it was all said and done, a jury of my peers only took **twenty minutes** to find me **NOT GUILTY** on all charges. The devil uses people, like this *Command Sergeant Major and others* to do his dirty work, and he try's his best to stop us, but God fought my battle and gave me the victory. They were really out to get me, but **Romans 8:31** says, *"...if God be for us, who can be against us."* Yes, it's costly to take a stand, but at least when I lay my head down at night, I know that I have stood for what is right. I know that my God will vindicate me whenever I stand, and plus I have given him a channel that he can use because the wrong needs to be righted. Even though it may cost you something to stand, our God is able and willing to deliver us, and he will deliver us, because right is right and wrong is wrong and wrong has to be dealt with.

As I was going through this ordeal, that was many things that my flesh wanted to do to help God out, but that's where we mess up. God doesn't need your help. I encourage you no matter what you're going through stand your ground and let the Lord fight the battle for you.

I believe with all my heart God saw my faith and integrity that day, that I would stand for what is right even a great personal cost. Six years later I was called and chosen by God to pastor. I was license and ordain and launched out into my own ministry, under the pastor that I got saved under in 1989. I believe God gave me an assignment that day that I was found not guilty, because I chose to stand for what was right even at great personal cost to my 17 year military career. He said to me, "you shall pastor and preach My gospel, **The Good News of Jesus Christ**, you shall proclaim the message of **Ethics and Integrity** to all that has an ear to hear". I encourage you to stand for what you know to be right even at great personal cost, because the battle is not your's, it's the Lord's, and he will fight it for you. God is always looking for someone that is full of faith, and have integrity that he can work his principles through. **Psalms 24:3–4** says, *"Who* *shall I ascend into the hills of the Lord? Or who shall stand in his holy place? He that hath clean hands, and a pure heart; who has not lifted up his soul unto vanity, nor sworn deceitfully."* So I will ask you this question, will that be you?

I heard the Lord say, **"FOR NOW HOLD YOUR PEACE** for the time will come when I will allow you to speak."

Chapter 3: My Dirt: Here Is My Wrongness

In this chapter, I talk about my wrongness as a young pastor, in the early years of my ministry, and how that wrongness hindered the growth and good success of my ministry, **until I made it right**. So I would like to start out by saying, your actions has consequences and you will never be able to prosper in your personal life, or in your ministry until you have made right the wrong that you have done, or done to others. In fact, you will begin to lose what you have, because God cannot allow you to continue to go forward and have good success in your personal life, or ministry until you have owned your wrongness. You might have a certain measure of success, but never on the level that God intended, because of your hidden sins. We find in **Matthew 5:23-24,** Jesus says, *"Therefore if thou bring thy gift to the altar, and there rememberest that thy brother hath ought against thee; Leave there thy gift before the altar, and go thy way; **first be reconciled to thy brother**, and then come and offer thy gift."* **Reconciled** means *to restore; to win over; to make up; to bring into agreement or harmony.* Noticed **the first thing** Jesus said to do, go to your brother **first** *(those who you have wronged)*, and be reconciled, then come and offer your gift or petition. If you have wronged others, I encourage you go to them, and apologize and ask them for forgiveness for the things that you have said, or done to them. Then go to God and ask Him to forgive you, because, you can't just bypass those people that you have wronged, and thank you can

35

just go straight to God, and he will forgive you. The order that Jesus gave is, go to the person **first**, that you have wrong, and ask for forgiveness, to restore harmony, and peace. **Then go to God**, and ask Him for forgiveness, and he will forgive you. I believe if you will do this, God will open doors for you beyond your dreams, exceedingly, abundantly, above, all that you can ask or think, and I believe that you will see a great change in your ministry, and life. You can't hide what you have done and expect to be blessed. That's what the modern-day Pharisee does, they do what they do, then cover, and hide it from the public eyes, and act like they've done no wrong. Unfortunately a lot of pastors do the same thing. In this chapter, I will also show you how you can be wrong in your sins, in those sins will stop your growth and good success, but as long as you own your sins, and stop hiding it, confess it to God, and make right to those you have wrong, and ask God to forgive you, He will. Once you do that, you will see a great change in your ministry. **Proverbs 28:13** says, *"He that covereth* (hide) *his sins shall not prosper: But whoso confesseth and forsake them* (to own it and turn from it) *shall have mercy."* God is waiting on you to stop hiding your sins, so he can show you mercy. God cannot show mercy to a person that refuses to own their wrongness, thinking they've done no wrong. If God showed you mercy while still in your hidden sins, that will send the wrong message to you, and that's why he will not show you mercy until you have owned your wrongness. I encourage you, go to those that you have wronged, and make it right, and ask God to forgive you, and He will, and He will show you mercy, and will bless you along your journey, **just as He did me**.

As I stated earlier, after seven years of serving under my pastor, he launched me out into my own ministry. I started my church in September 1997, in Fayetteville North Carolina where it remains to this day. In the early years (2000 or 2001) of the ministry there was certain things that I didn't know as a young pastor, and I made some major mistakes. So, before I talk about someone else's wrongness, their dirt, **here is my wrongness, my dirt**. I allowed people to get too close to me in ways that should not have been. This is my dirt and I own it; I allow one of my female members to walk up to me and kiss me on my lips. It was not a prolong kiss. It was only a smack, that's all it was, but a kiss is a kiss, and I allowed it, and I was wrong in every way. This is my dirt, and I own it. All was well until, months later, I had to correct the young lady on something else unrelated to the kiss, and she was embarrassed and offended. So, she blew the whole thing out of proportion to get back at me. Her and her husband emailed my pastor and embellished the story. The next month *(October 2001)* when my wife and I went to the men's conference at my pastor's church, and after the conference, my pastor talked to us about it. I explained that it did not happen that way. About a year later, the young lady and her husband, me and my wife, we all were at a funeral in Nashville Tennessee for a young man, that we all knew. After the funeral, we all had the opportunity to talk. The young lady and her husband came clean to my wife and I and said, "no, things didn't happen the way I said it to your pastor, I blew it up out of proportion because I was mad, embarrass and offended." She apologized to us, and I apologized to her and her husband, and that was the end of it. I heard that they moved to South Carolina, and to this day, we have never seen them again. I know people, and some of you that are reading this book think it was more to it than that, but you know what? You can think or believe what you want to think or believe, **because I don't care**. In twenty-seven years of pastoring, one thing I have learned about people and I'm talking about christians, church folks, some are quicker to believe the negative than the positive. And that's because, they want it to be what they want it to be, because if it were them, that's what they would have done. I've owned my wrongness, and I have confessed it. **I've repented from it, and my wife and God has forgiven me of it, and that's the only thing that matters**. I've learned, and you need to learn this also, that when you mess up, don't run from God, but run to Him, and He will receive you with love. **I don't fault the young lady, I only fault myself**. I failed that young lady, and God, and I have failed myself. One day that test, will come again, and when it does, I will be ready this time. This is my dirt, and I own it. I'm the pastor and judgment must always begin with me.

I also was talking to people and treating them in ways that was not done in love. This is also my dirt, and I own it. One day after church someone pulled me to the side and talk to me and said you don't have to talk to people in that way, nor treat God's people that way. You are not a drill sergeant anymore, and you are not in the military any longer. These are God's people, and you should treat them and talk to them with love and kindness. What that person said to me resonated with me that day, and I made a change, because I understood that change begins with me not someone else. From that day to this, I have always walked a straight and narrow path to treat and talk to people the way I would want to be treated and talk to.

I also, in December 2021, was very disrespectful to my pastor. Again, this is my dirt, and I own it. We *(my pastor and his wife, two other pastors, and my wife and I)*, were on zoom doing some teaching, and somehow the whole thing went sideways. My pastor started talking like he was so self-righteous saying, I have never done any wrong, I have always done right by you. When he said that, I totally lost it! I started bringing up to him, yelling, talking loud not in a nice way totally disrespectful, how you embezzled money and the earlier years of your ministry, and you use my wife and I to help you do that. Now, I shouldn't have done that, because that is sowing discord among brethren, and according to **Proverbs 6:19,** sowing discord is one of the seven things that the Lord hate. Whether it's right or wrong, true or false, good or bad, if you're spreading it to those that did not know, is sowing discord. You know why? By telling someone else's business, has now changed that person's perspective or feelings about that individual. So it doesn't matter whether it's true or false, by telling others that did not know, you are sowing discord, you have now put yourself on God's list of doing the things that He hate, according to **verse 16**. The other pastors didn't know anything about the embezzling, and I was wrong for bringing it up at that time. I talked about how you have hidden your actions of embezzling, even to this day. I went on to talk about, how you didn't come and support my wife and I on our new church building grand opening dedication service, simply because you thought you wasn't the guest speaker, and that was wrong of you. And you have the nerves to sit here and talk about you never done any wrong, and that you have always done right by me! I said, that's a bunch of junk! Now, I was totally out of line. I did it in front of my wife and two other pastors that was on zoom with us, I let my flesh take over and I was wrong in every way. After we hung up on zoom, the Holy Spirit said to me, now what do you think you're doing? Your pastor might be wrong, but you're just as wrong as he is. I immediately tried to call back, but they would not answer. So, I sent an email saying that I need to call back and apologize for my actions to everyone that was on zoom. My pastor's wife sent me an email back saying, call back in a week. I said in my email back to her, I just need to apologize today for my actions. She told me again, call back in a week. Now you might think why would she say call back in a week? I found out months later, this is what she did. She called the other two pastors that were on zoom with us at the time and got their story together how they were going to come after me when I call back, because of the way I acted. When I called back in a week on zoom, you could tell, that my pastor and his wife, and the other two pastors was loaded for bear. They were sitting there, ready to unload on me. My pastor talked for about fifteen minutes and then he said Pastor Williams has something to say. I had no intent to sit there and try to defend my actions or to justify my conduct, because I was wrong. When I was given the opportunity to speak, I said, I was wrong and every way, make no mistake about it, and I make no excuse for my action or conduct. There was no honor, and no respect in my actions. I didn't make any excuse. I said pastor I was wrong, in every way and I asked you to forgive me. I went to each person that was on zoom and told them I was wrong please forgive me, and I apologize for my actions, and then I looked at my wife and told her honey forgive me for sitting here last week, acting like a fool. I told them all, I was wrong and every way. After I apologize to everyone, looking at all of them on zoom, it look like the air went out of their balloons, to unload on me. They didn't expect to just hear me apologize; they were expecting me to give some kind of lame excuse for my actions a week ago. No, I was not going to give an excuse because excuses are satanic. Let me give you my definition of an excuse, and I pray that my definition will help you the readers to stop giving excuses. **An excuse** is; *"a Satanic explanation, that is given, to obtain a release, from a commitment, a responsibility, or a God-given obligation. In short, an excuse is for the uncommitted."* Vernon Brundage Jr said, *"excuses are the tools of incompetence use to build bridges to nowhere, and monuments of nothingness, and those who use them seldom specialize in anything else."* If you're not committed to your ministry, or to whomsoever God has placed over you, are what God has called you to do, the devil will always give you an excuse, a way out, and you will always specialize in nothing but excuses. Everyone said we accept your apology, and my pastor's wife said, let's move forward from this day and leave the past in the past. That's what she said, but she definitely did not mean it, because as time went on, she kept bringing up my past. That's all right, because this is my dirt, and I own it, all of it, every bit of it, I was wrong in every way. You might ask why would I tell on myself, why would I tell my personal business? I'll tell you why, a person of integrity will bear the consequences of their conviction, they're wrongness no matter how bad it was, even when this is difficult. **1 Peter 4:17** says, *"For the time is come that judgment **must** begin at the house of God: and if it first begin at us, what shall the end be of them that obey not the gospel of God?"* In other words, God is saying correction must began at the top. Obedience to God and what He has said, must begin with the pastors or those that are in leadership position. But what are we talking about in this book? The Modern-Day Pharisees: The Uncovering, how they hide their sins from the public eyes, to make themselves appear holy and righteous to others. But Jesus said in **Luke 16:15,** *"God knows their hearts."* So, for me to talk about other people's business, their wrongness, and not talk about my owns first, would make me a hypocrite. God always has a way of uncovering your sins. By the way, if you're wondering, did I record my stupid actions, yes, I did. I've done some things in my life that I am not proud of, and is a shame of, but I own them all. I make no excuse for my past actions, but I know God has forgiven me, because I have asked for forgiveness, and He has redeemed me from my past, and present wrongness, because he is the holder of my days to come. Everyday I can see His blessings on me, spiritually, physically, and financially. If He had not forgiven me, there's no way in this world I would have, or have done the things that I have done in my life, and are still doing. There is no way I could be blessed the way I am, and that's nobody, but God, and I give Him all the thanks, and praise. One thing I've learned in thirty-four years of ministry, and that is, **when God has a purpose for you, and you own your wrongness, and ask for forgiveness, even your mistakes, He will conform them, to complete His purpose through you**. But if you never own your sins, and ask for forgiveness, you have tied the hands of God and He cannot complete His purpose through you, and He will move on to someone else. Jesus said in **John 8:7** *"...he that is without sin among you, let him first cast a stone... ."* Stop judging others, as though you have no sins. **Romans 3:23** says, *"for all have sinned, and come short of the glory of God"*, and that means you also. Pastors, it's **NOT** the mistakes that we've done that defines us, but it's what we do **AFTER** the mistakes, <u>**is what defines us**</u>. I believe every mistake we make can be a learning process to grow and mature us, **IF** we have a heart to receive what the Holy Spirit has uncovered, and revealed. Those mistakes doesn't make us any less of a good person, but it's what we've learned from those mistakes, and have made the necessary, or proper corrections to never do that again, **that's what really defines us**. When you humble yourself, own and confess your sins, and ask for forgiveness, God will work through you, and do exceedingly, abundantly, above, all that you can ask, or think, and you will be amazed at what He has done through you.

One thing, my mother said and it helped to encourage me to continue on. She said, son everyone has some wrongness. What you have to do is own your wrongness and confess it to God and ask Him to forgive you and move on regardless of what people have to say or think. She said don't let what people say or think about you stop you from doing what God has called you to do. Praise God for that statement.

Now that you know these things about me, and that I am not perfect, and I have some wrongness, and have owned it, all of it, and it's going to play an important role about what I will go on to talk about in this book. Now, when you finish talking about the wrongness that I've done, make sure you don't forget to talk about the good that I've done also.

Let's move on.

Chapter 4: The Vision Began

In this chapter, I would like to show you how God open doors of good success for me as a pastor, **AFTER I got it right**, by owning and confessing my sins, and asking God to forgive me, and I made a change. Change always begins with you, and not someone else. Don't be like the modern-day Pharisee, hiding what they do from the public eyes, thinking they've gotten away with what they've done, but they have only deceived themselves. So I encourage you to own your sins just as I did in chapter three, and God will bless you along your journey in ways that is exceedingly, abundantly, above all that you can ask or think.

Habakkuk 2:2-4 says, *"And the Lord answered me, and said, Write the vision, and make it plain upon tables, that he may run that read it. For the vision is yet for an appointed time, but at the end it shall speak, and not lie: though it tarry, wait for it; because it will surely come, it will not tarry. Behold, his soul which is lifted up is not upright in him: but the just shall live by his faith."*

Pastors, and church leaders, God said, your vision is for an appointed time, that means it's not in your timing, it's in God's timing, and we have to learn to wait on God for His appointed time. God's appointed time for you is when you have matured enough to carry out the vision. He can't allow you to go forward with His vision if you are immature, because you will be puffed up with pride, and you will fail. God is a faith God and when it comes to our vision, we have to operate in faith, because faith is what pleases Him. God will show you your destiny, through vision, but never tell you how He's going to get you there, and there's a reason why, because your vision is a glimpse of your end, your destiny. Between your end and where you are, is called the plan. The plan is the process that takes you to your destiny. **Isaiah 46:9-10** says, *"...I am God, and there is none like me, declaring the end from the beginning, and from ancient times* **the things that are not yet done**, *saying, My counsel shall stand, and I will do all my pleasure."* God is letting us know there is no one like Him, He said, I look at the end, which is destiny, and I proclaim it from the beginning, which is vision. God will tell you your end, which is destiny, through vision, and back you up from the end, and start you out at your beginning. God will not tell you how He's going to get you to your end, which is your destiny, from the beginning. Between the beginning, which is vision, until the end, which is destiny, **there's a plan**. Now, isn't that something? God already has a plan for you, and this is what the LORD has to say about the plan that he has for you. He said in **Jeremiah 29:11** *"For I know the thoughts* (or the plans) *that I think toward you, saith the LORD, thoughts* (or plans), *of peace, and not of evil,* **to give you an expected end**.*"* Whether you know it or not, you have an expected end. He showed Joseph the throne, which is his expected end, and how his brothers will bow before him, and how he fed them during the time of famine, while sitting on the throne, and that was his end, his destiny. But God did not show him how he was going to get to the throne. God shows each and every pastor the end, which is destiny, through vision, but He never tell you or show you the plan, how He's going to get you there. You know why? **The plan is secret to God**. If He told you the plan, how he was going to get you there, and all you're going to go through, you would say, if I have to go through all of that, forget my destiny! The plan is to prepare you for your destiny. **The plan will take you through all the different changes, to develop you, to grow you, and to mature you**. When you go through things that is causing you to bend, as though it's breaking you, it's not. You won't break, just don't give up, because, what you don't realize is, what you're going through is actually making you stronger, and better. If Joseph had known he had to go through being hated by his brothers, put in a pit, sold into slavery, being lied on by Potiphar's wife, and put in prison to get to the throne, Joseph would have said, I'm not going through all of that, forget the throne. If Moses knew he had to go through all he went through, chased by Pharaoh, hated by the very people he brought out of Egypt, and they turned on him, even his own sister, wandering in the wilderness for forty years, and he get to the end of the journey, and God tells him, you can't go into the promised land, Moses would have said, forget the promised land, I'm good right here at the bottom of the mountain taking care of the sheep. **Your plan is always secret to God**, because if we knew what we had to go through to get to our destiny, we would say, if I got to go through all of that, forget it. God will not reveal the plan to you, He only shows you the destiny, because the plan is designed for you, **when, and only when, you have developed and matured and is ready to carry it out**. While serving in the military and in ministry, I have seen too many leaders that is not mature enough, or properly trained to handle certain jobs, and they fail at it, because they were not ready to handle it. Pastors, you can't give an immature person a difficult task and expect them to be successful at it, you are setting them up for failure, and discouragement in ministry. Right now you might not be where you want to be spiritually, but as you grow, and develop, God will reveal the next part of His plan to you, to get you to your destiny. Know this, the plan is always revealed in parts, so you can handle it, it will never be all at once. As Joseph and Moses went along their course of destiny, these things were revealed in parts, not all at once, so they were able to overcome, and handle whatever came up. **1 Corinthians 10:13** says, *"There hath no temptation* (trial or test), *taken you but such as is common to man: but God is faithful, who will not suffer* (or allow), *you to be tempted above that ye are able; but will with the temptation* (trial or test), *also make a way to escape, that ye may be able to bear it."* So you see here in the scripture that God would not allow anything to come upon you that he have not already equipped you to handle. If it comes upon you, that means you can handle it, because He said He would not allow it to come, if you couldn't. You have already been enabled, to handle whatever comes upon you, by standing in faith on what God has promised. If you are removed from your position as a leader, for whatever reason, or you lost all that you have, don't worry, is part of the plan. God is working on and preparing you for what He has prepared for you. A lot of leaders will never know what God has prepared for them, is because they are not willing to go through the process, of what it takes to develop, and mature themselves spiritually, they are always looking for a shortcut, and that's why they become man pleasers, and people pleasers. Change, and growth is never easy, there will always be naysayers, and critics, talking about what you can't do, but if you believe that you can succeed, you already have. **Pastors, your success in ministry is not measured by what you see, but rather it is measured by what you can believe God for.** Jesus said in **Mark 9:23**, *"If thou canst believe, all things are possible to him that believeth."* In the book of Mark chapter 5 it says, *"the ruler of the Synagogue came running to Jesus and fell at His feet and said, my little daughter lieth at the point of death, come home with me and lay thy hands on her, that she may be healed; and she shall live."* And the scripture says, Jesus went with him. And while Jesus was going with him, verse 25 and 29 says, there was a certain woman that had an issue of blood for twelve years, and she stopped Jesus in the midst of his travel, to the ruler of the Synagogue house. That little lady got a miracle by touching Jesus clothes, and Jesus told her, *"thy faith has made you whole."* Why did she get a miracle? I'll tell you why, **because she believed**. And in verse 35 it says, *"while he yet spake, there came from the ruler of the* *synagogue's house certain which said, thy daughter is dead: why troublest thou the master any further?* Verse 36 says, *as soon as Jesus heard the word that was spoken, he said to the ruler of the synagogue,* **be not afraid, only believe**." In other words, Jesus was telling him, don't doubt, only continue to believe what you were believing in the beginning, *"come home with me lay hands on her and she will be healed and live."* Jesus was telling the ruler of the Synagogue just keep on believing that. It goes on to say, in verse 41 and 42, *"Jesus took her by the hand and told her to arise,"* and she lived. It happened because the ruler of the synagogue kept on believing. So I will ask you this question, what can you believe God for? Stop being moved by what you see, on Sunday mornings, just a few members, because what you see is only temporary. **2 Corinthians 4:18** says, *"while we look not at the things which are seen, but at the things which are not seen: for the things which are seen are temporal; but the things which are not seen are eternal."* God is encouraging you, by letting you know, what you see right now, don't be moved by it, because if you don't give up, it is only temporary, and it is subject to change, and there are better days ahead. **Galatians 6:9** says, *"And let us not be weary in well doing: for in **<u>due season</u>** we shall reap, **<u>if we faint not</u>**."* Faint means to get weak and give up. God is letting us know, to never give up on what He has called you to do, or what you are believing him for. God wants us to continue to walk by faith, and not by sight, no matter what.

My wife and I stood in faith when we heard the

Holy Spirit say, I want you to move to the southwest side of town. Now mine you, the building that we were in, were paid for in full, but the area we were in was not a good part of town. There was crime, drugs, and prostitution. We had purchased this building a few years earlier and renovated it and over the years we had paid for it in full. We were debt-free, and we did it by faith. The year was 2004 and we only had about 75 members, and I heard the Lord say, I have some land for you on the southwest side of town, go buy it. I was going home one day, and I decided to go in a different direction when I left the church. As I drove down Bingham Drive on the southwest side of town, I passed by some land on the left of the highway. The Holy Spirit said to me, go to the courthouse and look up the owner of the property and contact them and buy that land. Mind you, there was no for sale sign on the property, but operating in faith and being led by the Holy Spirit, the next day I went to the courthouse and looked up the owner of the property. I called him and said, my name is Pastor Williams, and I am looking for land to build a new church. I know that there's no for sale sign on your land on Bingham Drive, but I was wondering are you interested in selling your land? After I said that, the owner started laughing and kept laughing, and finally he stopped and said Pastor Williams, I'm not laughing at you, but I'm laughing at what you just asked me. Am I interested in selling my land? He said you're not going to believe this, but just last night my wife and I talked about selling that piece of property and here you are calling me the very next day asking me am I interested in selling it? He said to me Pastor

Williams, that's nobody but the Holy Spirit. Yes, I'm interested in selling. To make a long story short, we *(our church)* bought 5 acres of prime property in a prime location on the southwest side of town for only $80,000. When you're standing in faith you know that's nobody but God. The problem I see with a lot of pastors is, they don't stand in faith. **Hebrews 11:6** says, *"But without faith it is impossible to please him: for he that cometh to God must believe that he is, and that he is a rewarder of them that diligently seek him."* According to this scripture when you go to God and ask for anything, you MUST ask in faith. It is an imperative, a necessity that whatever you do, must be done by faith. You don't have to go to God, you can try and do it yourself, but if you do go to God, it must be in faith. If you're not operating in faith, you're not pleasing God and if you're not pleasing God, there is no reward for you.

In 2014 God started really dealing with my heart about building the new church on the land that we had purchased ten years earlier on the southwest side of town. Over those ten years our membership grew and declined. It would go up and down, because we had a lot of soldiers, and they were deploying to war. The membership would grow to 205 members, go back down to 175 to 150 back up to 190 and finally down to 123 members. God gave me an assignment, and a vision, he said I'm going to use you to build a building debt-free, with just a handful of members to show that I'm still working in the earth realm today. I presented the vision to the congregation to build the new church debt-free, everyone said, we are with you pastor, we can do it, we can do it pastor, debt-free. I felt good about it that Sunday morning, all 123 members was with me. As I was praying one night, God spoke to me and said everyone who is saying we're with you pastor, we can do it, there heart is not with the vision to build debt-free. God told me to pray those out whose heart is not with the vision. Now let me stop and explain. I didn't get up in front of everyone and say, if your heart is not with the vision leave, I didn't do that. But what I did do, in my prayer time I prayed, Lord whoever's heart is not with the vision let them leave. I told my leadership this is how I want you to pray in your personal prayer time. Meanwhile I did my due diligence, sat down with contractors to find out, what is it going to cost to build a building that's 8400 square ft., that seats 300 people, three classrooms, nursery, fellowship hall, kitchen, and four offices, these are the things that we desired. I told the contractor I'm not trying to build to impress someone, or to be like someone else, or beyond my means. I am building what we need. I was told the cost would be $1.3 million. I said to myself, we have 123 members, we can do it. I was basing my decision on what I saw, 123 members. As we went on to pray throughout the year of 2014, we start watching the membership decrease every Sunday, it was less and less people at church. No pastor wants to see their membership decrease, we are always believing God for increase. By January 2015, the membership was down to 33 members, all the rest we had prayed out, so I thought. All those whose heart was not with the vision was gone. When God tells you to do something, he is telling you to do it for your own good, He is trying to get something to you. He knows the ending from the beginning, He knows whose heart is not with the vision, and who's heart is against change. Pastors, I said it before, and I'll say it again, change will never be easy, there will always be naysayers, but when you believe you can succeed, you already have. We now have 33 members, and I heard God say plainly now, go build the building and I'll be with you. I said God, go build the building? We have 33 members and only $65,000 in the bank, $1.3 million to build, and you saying, go build the building? **2 Corinthians 4:18** says, *"While we look not at the things which are seen, but at the things which are not seen: for the things which are seen are temporal; but the things which are not seen are eternal."* I was looking at what I saw, 33 members, only $65,000 in the bank, and I heard the Holy Spirit say, don't be moved by what you see, because what you see is only temporary. God was telling me to go do what He has already given me. God was showing me, that He is no respect of person. He said to me, if I can do it for Gideon, with only 300 soldiers and defeat a great army, I can do it for you. If you can believe, with only 33 members, and $65,000 in the bank, to build a $1.3 million church building debt-free, I can do it for you also. It's all about the principal, and the principal is the same as with Gideon. If I believe and trust God, He will also do it for me. I heard Him say to me again go build the building, I have given you favor among men.

Side note: I don't remember what year, but my

pastor wrote a book that is very good, but unfortunately I can't give you the title of the book without revealing his name. Remember the whole purpose of my book is that others may learn from my experience of being in ministry for thirty-four years. It is not meant to put anyone on blast or put them down by calling their name, the name of their church, or even the title of their book. I wish I could give you the title of his book, because it's really a good book, and my pastor should have published that book back then when he wrote it. Instead, he just had the book printed and sold them on his own. I believe if that book had been published at that time, it would have been a best seller. It's for sale on Amazon now, but I believe everything has a season and a time. To this day, I am still teaching from that book. That book made me free from walking into my church every Sunday morning counting people, waiting to do something until I had a certain amount of people. God is a faith God, and faith is what pleases Him. Faith in God is what should move us, and not what we see.

God said to me, three things I require of you while building this building. He said: **Number one:** *take no speaking engagements while building this building.* **Number two:** *you be on site with the contractors everyday.* **Number three:** *give, you and your wife and the church like you've never given before, and I'll be with you all the way.* Let me explain why God told these three things that was required of me. **Number one: *"take no speaking engagements."*** If I had taken speaking engagements, I would've been in my office studying and not on site with the contractors every day as God said to do. **Number two:** *"you be on site with the contractors every day."* Well, that goes back to number one. If I had taken speaking engagements, I wouldn't have been on site every day with the contractors. The reason why God told me to be on site with the contractors every day was, He had given me favor with men, and if I was not here on site every day when the favor came, I would have missed it. *(later I'll explain the favor more)*. Pastors that's where we miss it at, we don't do the part that we can do, that God tells us to do. Like be on site with the contractors every day, that's the easy part. Instead, we make excuses, and not do the simple things that we can do. God is waiting on you to do the part that you can do, which is the easy part, and in return, God will do the part we can't do, which is the hard part, like giving you favor with others. **Number three:** *"give, you and your wife and the church like you've never given before."* We did that because we understood through the taught word of God, that God is never trying to get something from you, He is always trying to get something to you, in this case for us, $1.3 million. *(later I will explain more why God told my wife and I and the church to give like we've never given before)*. In order for God to get finances to you, you going to have to sow finances. **Galatians 6:7** says, *"...for whatsoever a man soweth, that shall he also reap."* That's in anything, whatever you sow that's what you're going to get in return. To make a long story short, June 2015 we broke ground and went forward with what we had. The concrete slab was poured. The metal framing went up. The outside shall of the building was installed, and the roof was put on. Each member pledged a certain amount of money by a certain time to move to the next phase. The money came in, and we framed the entire inside of the building. On the last day of framing, all of the workers had completed their work and left. It was in my spirit to stay and pray. As I was walking through the building praying, a white guy came through the door and said, hey! Are you the pastor? I said yes, he said you're not going to believe this, he said God sent me here to help you build this building. I said man you know how many times I've heard that? He said no I'm serious, I tried my best not to stop here. I passed by and the Holy Spirit said to me, go back and help that pastor build that building. I turned around and came back but did not stop, I passed on by again and the Holy Spirit dealt with me and said, go over and help that pastor build that building. To make a long story short, I found out later while talking to this guy, he was wealthy. He didn't look the part, he didn't act the part, and he didn't talk the part, but he was wealthy. One thing I know for sure, he was God sent, everything we needed he knew how to get it at a reduced price. He has so much favor in this town that all he would do is make a phone call and whatever material we need, it was delivered the next day sometime the same day. He is the owner of his own heating and air company *(I won't give the name of the company or his name for his privacy)*. He also is co-owner of his own electrical company. He owned two restaurants in North Myrtle Beach, South Carolina, and if you know anything about North Myrtle

Beach, that's money. He also owned two restaurants in Miami, Florida, the guy was wealthy. Now, *this is that favor that I told you earlier that I will talk to you more about later*. Listen to this. He knew where to get anything we needed; workers included at a reduce labor cost. He said you don't have to wait and raise the money, he said I'll pay for it, and you all just raise the money and pay me later. He had his heating and air company to install our complete heating and air system for the building at a cost of $117,000 completed, we paid not a penny down. He also had his electrical company to do all of the electrical work at a cost of $77,000 completed, we paid not a penny down. Again, he said just raise the money and pay me later, and I will not charge you any interest. Look at God's favor, what a blessing. The next phase was installing sheet rock. **Then I messed up**. A good pastor friend of mine passed away unexpectedly. I used to speak at his men's conference, and he used to speak at mine. When he passed away, his son took over the men's conference, and asked me because he knew I was his dad's good friend, would I come speak at the men's conference? Remember what God told me, *"take no speaking engagements."* I told him yes, I'll be there, and I took my men with me also. Pastors, and church leaders, sometimes we do things thinking it's ok, because of death was involved, but if God told you not to do something, that's exactly what He means, don't do it. The men's conference took place on that Saturday morning, and that Saturday evening I get a call from the contractor saying, next week we won't be out during the work, because we have another job to do. To make a long story short, four months had past, with no work taking place on the site because of my disobedience. No money was coming in, also six members left, leaving us with 27 members, and there was no favor. So, I let my flesh get involved, my own way of thinking, and I go out and buy a lottery ticket. Now, isn't that's crazy, a foolish way of thinking. Thinking that I'm going to win the lottery and build the building that God said He was going to build debt-free. To be honest, I don't know what I was thinking, I guess I can say I wasn't thinking rationally. Do you think God is going to use the tool of the devil to do his work? Let me answer that question for you, no He's not! I went out to the building the next day to pray, and as I was walking through the building, sheet rock dust all in my hair, all on my eyebrows, and all over my clothes I was looking like a snowman. I said Lord, what is going on, why the money is not coming in? Why are the workers not out here working? God said because of your disobedience. God reminded me of what he said, *"take no speaking engagement while building this building."* I said, Lord, forgive me, what must I do to make it right? God said, now go stand before your people and tell them what you've done. Pastors, this is the part we don't want to do when we are wrong. We want to hide what we have done, but don't want to admit openly when we are wrong, and that's what stops your blessing. This is how the modern-day Pharisee operate in this day and time. Doing the same things that they did in Jesus' time, hiding their sins, but exposing the people sins openly. What did Jesus call them? Hypocrites!

They always want to hide what they've done from the people and make themselves look spiritual. But expose the people when they are wrong. **1 Peter 4:17** says, *"For the time is come that judgment must begin at the house of God: and if it first begin at us, what shall the end be of them that obey not the gospel of God?"* Pastors, for the ministry that we are over everything, judgment and blessings, starts and end with us. Remember **Proxerbs 28:13** says, *"He that covereth* (hide) *his sins shall not prosper... ."* So, Sunday morning, I stood before the people that God has placed me over and told them all that I had done. I told them, I disobey God and took a speaking engagement, when he told me not to. Not only did I do that, but I also went and bought a lottery ticket thinking that I was going to win and use the money to finish building the building, and that's why our blessings and favor has been cut off. I disobeyed God and I was wrong and every way, and I asked you all to forgive me. That's how I said it, and I didn't go and try and sweeten or clean it up and make it sound or look good, or all spiritual. I told them the truth. That was at our Sunday morning service, that Sunday evening I got a phone call from the contractor, and he said can you have the gate open by 5:30 AM tomorrow morning? We will be there working. Not only did the workers start back Monday morning, also later that week we got a large financial donation. God turned the whole situation around overnight, I said overnight, because I as the pastor confess my sin, turn from it and got it right. When God says He's going to do a thing, that means He's going to do it, and don't try to help God out. The rest is history, the building was built with 27 faithful members that stood in faith until the end. At the completion of the building, we did not pay $1.3 million to build it. We only paid $800,000 for a building valued at $1.3 million to build. God did it, and God blessed us with it. We saved $500,000 doing it Gods way. Look at what God did, not us, but God, debt-free, PAY FOR IN FULL, favor. Remember the building that we were in, on the other side of town, that we had purchased some years earlier and renovated it. We purchased that building for $175,000. God blessed us when our new building was finished, we sold that building for $375,000, favor, once again, what a blessing. We give Him the thanks, and the Praise! Now, some of you might be wondering how much my pastors donated. In February 2016 when my pastor, was here in North Carolina visiting, to take care of some personal business, and to check out the progress of the work, he said his church would donate $1000. And he did, but it took him three years and seven months to send it. He had gotten upset with me because of something that I asked him while he was here. Now mind you, we were raising money and paying for all the work as we went, so we needed the money right away, as soon as possible, (ASAP)! Well, I just thank God, we got it eventually.

Remember, I told you that I would discuss more later about *"giving like we've never given before."* Well, here it is. I said, the third thing that God told me was to give, my wife and I and the church like we've never given before. Doing those four years and nine months of building the new church, my wife and I, personally gave unto my pastor and his wife, not their church, but them personally, $40,725. And my church gave to my pastor's church, $72,000. The grand total of giving was $112,725 total, doing the four years and nine months of building of our new church building. Now you might say, wow! Why would you do that, while raising money to build a new church as you go? Why would you give away that kind of money? That's what some of the other pastors asked me when I told them how we were giving. I told them, God told me to do it. They said man, you shouldn't do that! They said, pastor, you should keep that money for yourself, to help with what you are doing. I couldn't listen to other people and let my flesh get involved, I had to do what I believe God told me to do. When you let your flesh get involved versus doing what God has told you to do, in spite of how you feel, you will miss your blessings. I did it because God told me to do it. Paul said in **1 Corinthians 9:27** *"But I keep under my body, and bring it into subjection...".* Anytime your flesh, your body, or you're thinking wants to get out of line with what God has told you to do, you, *(the spirit man)* have to bring it back under control. **2 Corinthians 10:3-5** says, *"For though we walk in the flesh, we do not war after the flesh: For the weapons of our warfare are not carnal, but mighty through God to the pulling down of strong holds, Casting down imaginations, and every high thing that exalteth itself against the knowledge of God, and bringing into captivity every thought to the obedience of Christ."* Now, look at the end results when you obey God. A $1.3 million building paid in full with 27 faithful members, that only cost us $800,000, to build, and saving us $500,000 in the process. That's, nobody but God. Remember, I told you, God is always trying to get something to you, and not from you. **Galatians 6:7** says, *...for whatsoever a man soweth, that shall he also reap."* What you sow, is what you're going to reap, or get back in return. If you need finances, then you have to sow finances in order to get finances in return. Those of you that is reading this book, I pray this help you. **Isaiah 55:8-9** says, *"For my thoughts are not your thoughts, neither are your ways my ways, saith the Lord. For as the heavens are higher than the earth, so are my ways higher than your ways, and my thoughts than your thoughts."* God thoughts and His ways are far higher than ours, and that's why it's important that we learn to trust Him in what we are doing, or what He has called us to do, no matter of our thoughts, our feelings, or what anyone have to say.

I would like everyone to know this. God bless us to build this building, and we sold no chicken dinners, no barbecue plates sales, no fish fried dinners, no bake sales, no candy sales, no cookie sales, no car washes, no fundraisers, no monthlong revivals, and no famous guest speakers coming in to raise any money for us. We did it all God's way, through the members tithes, offering, pledges, and donations. Praise the Lord!

Chapter 5: **Grand Opening Service**

As I stated earlier, we started work in June 2015, and the building was completed March 2020. It took four years and nine months to complete but paid for in full with 27 faithful members. Unfortunately, upon completion, the pandemic hit, *(Covid-19)* and the nation was shut down for a whole year. We did not hold our first service and our new building until fifteen months later.

Listen closely to what I'm about to say and see if you can spot the modern-day Pharisee in what I am saying. Remember, they are all about themselves, and no one else. When the nation opens back up after the pandemic, we were so excited about our new building, we wanted to start holding services as soon as possible. We held our first service on June 13, 2021, fifteen months after the building was completed. We advertise for three months that we will be holding our new church building Grand Opening service, on Saturday, August 21, 2021, at 12 PM. We did it that way so that people that was coming from out of town would not have to rush to get here. They can celebrate with us for about two hours on Saturday and have time to leave and go back home for their own church services on Sunday if they so desired, or they could stay in fellowship with us on Sunday morning also. While building the new building in February 2016, my pastor came to visit to take care of some personal business, and to see the progress of the work. I told him while he was here, I would like for him to be the guest speaker for our grand opening service, he said OK. Two years later, in 2018, my pastor was holding a men's conference at a church south of Atlanta Georgia, and my wife and I was there in attendance. While there the Lord spoke to me and said, tell your pastor, **the Lord said**, *"that I will speak my own grand opening service."* So, I did, and my pastor said sure, because nobody can thank the people that gave like you can, only you know the vision, and only you know who gave. I was surprised he took it that calmly with me face-to-face, but I was in for a big surprise and a very rude awakening. When he got back home, he called me up, and totally lost it! Him and his wife went off on me with vengeance, because he was not the guest speaker. They were angry and called me everything but a child of God. I tried to talk, I said, pastor that's not what you said in Atlanta when you were there. You said, ok, that's fine, because no one can thank the people the way I could because you are the only one know who gave. I said that's what you said, why couldn't you tell me at that time that you were displeased with that decision? I was told to stop talking, and just listen, so I did. **And that's where the problem lies with my pastors, and with abusive leaders**, you never get the opportunity to complete your statement before you are cut off, and told to stop talking, and just listen. So I stopped talking, and at this point started recording. Now do you really think talking to me or treating me that way is going to get me to change my mind, and let you be the guest speaker? No it will not! As a leader, this is a domineering leadership style, and it is very offensive, and is should not be, because it always sends the wrong message. It is saying to the person that is trying to talk to their leader, what you have to say to me is not important enough for me to listen to you, but what I have to say to you, is more important than what you have to say to me, so just shut-up and listen. That's a sad place to be as a leader, because effective communication is a two-way street. It's a dialogue, you talk and I listen, then I talk and you listen. But with a selfish leader, is always a monologue, it's only about what they have to say, and don't care about what you have to say. Don't be this type of leader, because the LORD said in **Isaiah 1:18** *"Come now, and let us reason together… ."* Meaning, let's sit down and have a dialogue and discuss this thing together. I encourage you to check my website from time to time for the releasing of these recordings that I made, if I decide to release them, and you will be able to hear for yourself how we have been talked to and treated over the years. In secret my pastors are the type of people that talk to you and treat you any kind of way, but in public they are totally a different person as though they are so caring. I am talking about the modern-day Pharisee how they appear to be righteous, holy and caring but yet they hide their actions from the public. My pastors have turn into someones that I could not recognize anymore, who do they deals in secret, very abusive and talk to the people any kind of way in secret, but in front of people act so holy. So, I shut up, and I just listen from that point and kept recording. God always has a plan, and His plan was to show me my pastors, *(him, and his wife)* true heart, how, it's all about themselves. This is how the modern-day

Pharisee operate in this day and time. It's all about themselves, it's all about their will and desires being force upon others. When it was time for the grand opening, I invited my pastors to come, but because he was not the guest speaker, **so he thought**, he and his wife said they were not coming. My pastor's wife told me, we are not going to pay out that kind of money to fly round-trip to come there to North Carolina to hear me, or anyone else speak, because her husband should be the guest speaker. She told me it is a dishonor and disrespectful for my pastor not to be the guest speaker. I told him I'm sorry he felt that way, but I told him what God told me to tell him, that I will speak my own opening service. She told me that's a lie, God has never told me that. I asked her how does she know what God told me? I told her she might be a prophetess, but she is not all knowing, and she has no idea what God has said to another person. I told her, I have now been pastoring for twenty-five years, do you really think God does not speak to me, or through me? But what are we reading about in this book, the modern-day Pharisees, The Uncovering, how is all about themselves and no one else. I told them I believe it's a dishonor, and it's disrespectful to God, for them to be our pastors, our covering, our spiritual father and mother, and they didn't come and honor what God has done through us. Now that's what I call betrayal. My pastor's wife had the nerve to talk about betrayal in one of her teachings! What a hypocrite! Lest see, lest talk about betrayal! I will show you, betrayal! Betrayal is when you've been with your pastors for thirty-four years and you have pastored under them for the last twenty-five of those thirty-four years. You've been faithful and has done everything that was asked of you by them. And God has blessed you, me and my wife to build a $1.3 million brand new church building debt-free, pay for in full, with 27 faithful members. Upon completion of your new $1.3 million building, that is paid for in full, you hold a grand opening building dedication celebration service to honor God for what He has done, not us, but what God has done. And your pastors who you've been with all these thirty-four years, does not come to support you and your grand opening celebration dedication service, because they are mad at you because they're not the guest speaker, **so they thought**. Now mind you, God told me to tell my pastor two years earlier, that I will speak my own grand opening service. I don't understand how you can come from another country, to the states, throughout the years, to support what other pastors are doing, but you would not come and support what your own pastors has done, that's been under you faithfully, for thirty-four years. How is it that you can be so spiritual, and as our pastors, allow yourselves, to get so mad, or be so self-righteous, you don't come, and support us, on what we have done, but yet come, and support what other pastors are doing. My pastor told me, he was coming, but when he asked his pastor friends about this, they said that's not right, you should be the guest speaker, **and I wouldn't go if I were you**. My pastor told me at that point is when he decided he was not coming. God showed my pastor, the right thing to do, to come and support us, but he allowed man to turn his heart, by saying, *"if I were you, I wouldn't go."* What a shame! Now, what those pastors should have said to him was, **pastor you're wrong.** That's your spiritual son in the ministry for thirty-four years, and whether you're the guest speaker or not, you should still be there to support them because that's what a good leader would do. But instead they said, *"if I were you, I wouldn't go."* When you lack integrity, you will always lead with your mouth, and not with your heart, and give the wrong advice. I don't understand why pastors won't open their mouth, and tell other pastors that they are wrong, when they see it. I'll tell you why I believe they won't. These are pastors that are trying to maintain favor with each other, so they can continue to speak at each other's church. This is what I call being man pleasers among each other, and betrayal to us! These are pastors that's operating in the sin of omission, they know the right thing to say, but they deliberately omit the truth. **James 4:17** says, *"Therefore to him that knoweth to do good, and doeth it not, to him it is sin."* When you know the right thing to say or do but refuse to do it, God still calls it sin. Pastors and leaders, I encourage you to stand up and be the man or woman that God has called you to be. When you see or hear something wrong say something, and do something, because people will lie and hide what they do to include pastors and leaders. When it comes to your fellow pastor or leader be the person of integrity and speak up, because remaining silent is consent. Don't be a man pleaser or a butt kisser! Man up and be God's mouthpiece and be the leader that He has called you to be regardless of the consequences. **Now, on my program, my order service for the grand opening service, <u>because of honor</u>, I had listed my pastor on the program as the guest speaker, but he didn't know that.** I was hoping he would show up, I was going to give him the honor position to be the speaker, if he had shown up. My pastors has trained us to always be ready to speak when you go someplace, because you never know how the Spirit of the Lord would move, so I knew if he came unaware that he would be the guest speaker he would be ready, because that's how he trained us. By my pastors, and the other covenant pastors, not coming to support us, **they made it all about <u>themselves</u>, and not about God**. It was no longer about coming to give honor, thanks, and praise for what God has done, it was more about self glorification, being the guest speaker, and man pleasers to each other. My pastor's wife said, "if my husband is not the guest speaker, we are not coming." I found out later that the other covenant pastors were encouraged not to go and support us, because it is a dishonor for your pastor not to be the guest speaker. It is a sad place to be when you have gotten to the point where you can't be happy for others, but you think that everything is always about you, and that you have to be out front in the spotlight. I understand now why God told me to tell my pastor that I would speak my own opening service. God already knew his heart that if he wasn't the speaker, he wasn't coming. **<u>God had to show that to me, and others</u>**. I know that because later the next week, after the grand opening and I talk to my pastors, and I told them how disappointed and how hurt we were, that they didn't come and celebrate an honor what God had done with us. His wife went off on us once again and said, no! We did not come, and we were not coming and spend that kind of money to fly round-trip **to hear you or anybody else speak**. If my husband is not the guest speaker, that is a dishonor, that is disrespectful, and that it was no honor for your pastor. I went on to tell them, if they had come, he would have been the guest speaker. I would have given you the honor position, you have never in twenty-five years of you coming to North Carolina and I have never not given you the honor position to speak. We were on zoom at the time I was talking to them, so I held up my program, order of service, and showed him that I had him down as the guest speaker, your name, if you just had showed up. He asked me why I didn't show that to him before or tell him he was the guest speaker. He told me, **If I had told him that, or showed him that, he would have come**. I told him, I know, **that's God's point**, and that's my point, you would only come if you was the guest speaker. I told you what God told me to tell you, because God wanted me to see your true heart. It's all about you out in front of the people speaking, and being seen. I've been with you for thirty-four years, why couldn't you just come and support us even if you wasn't the guest speaker, because that's what love would have done. Pastors, everything is not always about you, sometime it's about others, and the love you should show them. Now that's the modern-day Pharisee in this day and time, doing things to be seen, by others. My pastor started laughing and making a joke out of it and said, "oh! Ha ha so, you tested me huh, you tested me." He did just as the Pharisee did when they heard what Jesus said, pointing out they're wrongness and correcting them in **Luke 16:14-15,** which says, *"And the Pharisees also, who were covetous, heard all these things: and **they derided him**. And he said unto them, **Ye are they which justify yourselves before men**; but God knoweth your hearts: for that which is highly esteemed among men is **abomination in the sight of God**."* Now, look at what the Pharisees did when they heard what Jesus said in **verse 14,** *"they derided Him."* **Derided** means, *"to laugh at in scorn or contempt; or to mock."* Remember what I told you about the modern-day Pharisee early in this book, they are all about themselves, and no one else. **So my pastor laughed, and mock me when I told him what God told me to tell him, and said, "ha ha so, you tested me huh, you tested me."** I told him no, I didn't test you, **God did!** I wanted you to come because you wanted to come and support us, not just because you're the guest speaker. What a shame! After he saw and heard this, I believe he realized that he had made a big mistake by not coming, and that he should've came. He didn't know how to come back from that. To this day, because of pride, he has never apologized, never said I'm sorry, never said I was wrong and never said I should've been there, despite my feelings. He really believed that he had done no wrong, by not coming and supporting us, **and honoring what God had done.** Now that's pride! Instead for the next year and a half they came after my wife and I with vengeance trying to run us out the ministry. Pastors stop running people off, and dismissing them because you don't want to pastor or shepherd them. Listen to what God says in **Jeremiah 23:1&2** says,*"Woe be unto the pastors that destroy and scatter the sheep of my pasture, saith the LORD. Therefore thus saith the LORD God of Israel against the pastors that feed my people; Ye have scattered my flock, **and driven them away**, and have not visited them: behold, **I will visit upon you the evil of your doings, saith the LORD**"*. Pastors and leaders, God is letting you know, that there will be a day of reckoning, there will be a day that you will given an account for your actions. When you dismiss people for whatever reason, you as the pastor are scattering the sheep, and are refusing to shepherd them, and you have failed at your job as a pastor. People are not fools to just believe everything you say. Oh yes, you might have the occasion, man pleaser, or butt kisser among you, but most people that hear you talk about dismissing or releasing this person or that person because they just wouldn't do right, know that is not always true. Believe it or not, your members will actually reach out to those people that you dismissed to find out what really happened, like they did my wife and me. They might not ever say anything to you about it, but they know the truth, and the only reason you dismissed them, is because they knew what you have been doing in secret. Your members know that you the pastor is lying, and is really the problem, by hiding what you have been doing. Pastors, stop dismissing people, and turning your back on them, and stop lying on others, saying they just wouldn't do right, and that's why you refuse to shepherd them, which is a lie. <u>So what if they won't do right</u>! **Stay the course, and shepherd them**, because turning your back on them, or dismissing them is just an excuse not to do your job, and that's satanic. **1 Thessalonians 5:14** says, *"...warn them that are unruly, **...be patient toward all men.**"* A good leader will always learn to be patient with others, and find a way to reach them, because turning your back on them, or dismissing them is not the fix. Did Jesus turn his back on you, when you were in your sins, and wouldn't get right? No he didn't! He had patient with you until you got right. Well, why turn your back on others, you must learn to operate with patient when it comes to others, and seek the Holy Spirit on how to shepherd them. Jesus did not say it will be easy to pastor people, he said *"my yoke is easy and my burdens are light"*. Paul called these things, light afflictions, and you, as pastors need to also view these things when they come up in your ministry as light afflictions. Pastors, I encourage you to continue to do what God has called you to do, and that is to shepherd, and feed the sheep, and feed the lamb, and not run them off. **Ezekiel 3:17-18** says, *"Son of man, I have made thee a watchman unto the house of Israel: therefore hear the word at my mouth, and give them warning from me. When I say unto the wicked, Thou shalt surely die; and thou givest him not warning, nor speakest to warn the wicked from his wicked way, to save his life; the same wicked man shall die in his iniquity;* ***but his blood will I require at thine hand.****"* God is saying to you pastors, I have set you as a shepherd, a watchman over my flock, feed them and warn them for me, and not run them off. If you don't warn them for me, and they die in their sins, because you have ran them off, **I will hold you accountable**. God is warning you, and letting you know pastors, you will not get away with anything, no matter who you are, or what your title is, there will be a day of judgment.

So, my pastors came up with the idea, that we pastors, need some retraining, training that we never got in the first place. So, after twenty-five years of pastoring, they started having all of us pastors, to meet with them on zoom every Monday morning at 7 AM, having each one of us pastors taking turns reading scriptures, like we are in elementary school having reading 101. They were treating us like we are pastors that's just starting out, and need someone to hold our hands. All of a sudden, after twenty-five years of pastoring, now they want to try to teach us how to pastor. It's a shame to treat season pastors in this way! I told them it's a little late for this, we've been pastoring now for twenty-five years, and this is an insult! This is like waiting to a child get to the 12th grade and now you're going to try and teach him or her their ABCs. Because you didn't take the time to teach that child earlier, they learned their ABCs through trial and error and other ways, that's how that child got to the 12th grade. I said we don't need this, not now. We needed this twenty-five years ago, but unfortunately, we didn't get it. Now, to my pastors' defense, we didn't have this technology twenty-five years ago, *(zoom and Facebook messenger)*, so, we couldn't do it this way. Again, like I said, you're trying to teach us how to be pastors now? We've learned it through trial and error, and I believe that God has made us very successful at it, and this level of leadership is very poor, and very offensive. My wife and I knew that we had outgrown our pastors in many areas, but we would never ever say that to them, we just remain humble. Everybody can't handle your growth, because your growth exposes their comfort zone. If your leaders can't handle your growth, it's time for you to move on, because they will become a problem for you. When you have outgrown your leaders, they will become jealous of what you do or have done, and they will try and keep you in a box to control you. **Whenever your light, outshine their light, <u>that's a problem for them</u>**, because you are now out of the box that they built to keep you in, and they will always find fault in everything you do. Don't let people keep you in a box, because God has enlarged your borders, and you are supposed to do bigger and better things. Now, I know you don't need a college degree to be called by God to preach the gospel, but God has blessed my wife and I to earn our doctorate degrees. Please listen, I'm not bragging, I'm just giving a good report of what the Lord has done for us. There's a different between bragging versus a good report. So let me explain. If I say, look at what I did, I took 27 members and I built a $1.3 million church building debt-free all by myself, or I say I got my doctorate degree all by myself no help from anyone, and not acknowledging God at all, now that would be bragging. But when I say **look at what**

God did, He took 27 faithful members in build a $1.3 million church building debt free, and I say God did it, not me, that would be a good report. Or I say, God blessed my wife and I, to manage our time in such a way, to be able to complete our doctorate degree, while raising a family, and pastoring the church. That would be a good report, because you're giving all the credit of your success to God. Through our higher education, the Holy Spirit has used it, and have showed us how to overcome, and learn through the trials and errors. That's a good report. God allows us to go through trials, and test, to grow and to mature us. Some things you can't learn until you physically go through them yourself, but I truly believe some things you can learn by another person's example. Don't do like that man or woman, you see what happened to them. My pastors, by their own admission, said all we have is a high school education and we are fine with that, we don't need anything else. If all you want is a high school education, that's fine, but don't put down the next person because they desire more. A college degree does not mean that you are all knowing. You are not called into the five-fold ministry out of the classroom just because you have a degree. The classroom only helps to sharpen and hone your skills as a pastor or leader. But I do believe that a college degree will help you a great deal along your journey from unseen pitfalls.

Chapter 6: **Everyone Has Some Wrongness**

Let me start by saying this, you have heard about my wrongness in chapter three, and I make no excuses for my actions, I own it, all of it. I don't care who you are, what title you may have, or what position you may hold, it doesn't matter, everyone has some wrongness, and **no one is above accountability**. So, let's talk about The Modern-Day Pharisees: The Uncovering, and how they do their deals in secret, have no accountability, and hide their wrongness from the public, but quick to expose others. Pastors, the problem I've seen over the years with leaders, is that even when they are caught in their wrongness, they refuse to own it. They try to lie their way out of it, by putting the blame on someone else, to take the focus off themselves, and that's called deflecting. You as a leader, that is under your leader, IF, you tell your head leader, the truth about themselves, about their wrongness, what they are doing, or not doing, your time is limited under them. Do you know why? You have now cast light upon their wrongness, what they are, or have been doing, and they will reject you, or anyone, that will highlight their wrongness. That's the life of the modern-day Pharisee to hide their wrongness, from the public's eyes, and get rid of anyone that will not agree with what they are doing, and that's why your time will be limited. It will be just a matter of time, before they devise a plan to get rid of you, or try an destroy your reputation. Pastors, we should tell each other the truth when we see each doing wrong, and don't lie to each other, trying to maintain favor. If the truth can't keep us together, then maybe, we don't need to be together. God sees and knows what you're doing, and he can't allow you to prosper or be successful.

Romans 3:23 says, "for *all have sinned, and come short of the glory of God."* Everyone has some wrongness, there is no one around you that is perfect, **including you!** My wrongness might be greater than your's, and your's might be greater than the next persons', but wrong is wrong and it has to be dealt with. In the eyesight of God, there is no big sin or little sin. Sin is sin and sin have to be dealt with. **1 John 1:8-10** says, *"If we say that we have no sin, we deceive ourselves, and the truth is not in us. If we confess our sins, he is faithful and just to forgive us our sins, and to cleanse us from all unrighteousness. If we say that we have not sinned, we make him a liar, and his word is not in us."*

I would like to quote one of our great faith, teachers, and authors, Dr. Frederick K.C. Price and read these scriptures the way he would read them. *"If we say that we have no sin,* **("when we know that we have sinned")**, *we deceive ourselves, and the truth is not in us. If we confess our sins, he is faithful and just to forgive us our sins, and to cleanse us from all unrighteousness. If we say that we have not sinned,* **("when we know we have sinned")**, *we make him a liar, and his word is not in us".* Man, that's powerful how he puts it! When you say you have no sin or wrongness, when you know you have sin and wrongness, you only deceive your own self, and you make God a liar, and the scripture says *"God is not a man that he should lie."*

God is long suffering, and has great mercy, and He is waiting on you to own and confess your sin. You can never prosper the way God intended you to prosper until you make it right. **Proverbs 28:13** says, *"He that covereth* (hide) *his sins shall not prosper: But whoso confesseth and forsake them* (to own it and turn from it) *shall have mercy."* God was right there when you were doing the sin, nothing is hidden from Him. He is waiting on you to stop hiding your sins, go to those that you have wronged, and make it right, and confess your sins and ask God to forgive you. **Matthew 5:23-24** says, *"Therefore if thou bring thy gift to the altar, and there rememberest that thy brother hath ought against thee; Leave there thy gift before the altar, and go thy way; **first be reconciled to thy brother**, and then come and offer thy gift."* **Reconciled** means *to restore; to win over; to make up; to bring into agreement or harmony.* I believe God is saying in these scriptures, how dare you, bring any kind of offering to Me, or to ask a petition of Me and you have not made right or restored harmony with your brother, it will not happen. The devil has blinded your mind to think that you can treat people anyway you see fit and think that God will still bless you. **Habakkuk 1:13** says, *"Thou art of purer eyes than to behold evil, and canst not look on iniquity... ."* If God cannot look on iniquity, which means evil doing, how do you think He's going to bless you, He can't! The

Modern-Day Pharisees: The Uncovering, is all about the uncovering of hidden sin, the exposing of wrongness in leadership today. You might think you know people, but you really don't, until they have been uncovered, because everyone has some wrongness. God gives us all the opportunity to uncover ourselves, meaning to stop hiding our sins, and own our wrongness, and turned from it, but if you don't, when God uncovers you with a public fall from grace, everyone is going to know about it. So stop hiding your sins before it's too late, and go get it right with those you have wronged.

In January 2001 my wife and I started going back-and-forth to my pastor's church in another country twice a year, January for the women's conference and October for the men's conference. Sometimes we are asked to speak and other time we are asked to teach a workshop. But teaching or not, we were always faithful to do what is asked of us. We went back-and-forth to my pastor's church for twenty-two years most times at our own expense, in another country. Let me say this, when we first started going to my pastor's church, if me and my wife were scheduled to be a guest speaker, our pastors would cover all expenses, airplane tickets, hotel cost and meals and given an honorary. But after a few years, all that stopped. You had to pay your own airplane ticket and they will cover the hotel cost and the meal even if you were the guest speaker and no honorary were given. In 2006 or 2007 Satan began to test my integrity once again. I begin to see things done by my pastor and others that lacked integrity. Again, a test of my integrity just as I experienced in the military, but I said this is church, and this has got to be different, so I thought. I wanted to question those things, but as a young pastor I thought I was supposed to see it, and not see it, hear it, and not hear it, and just do what you're told, because that's my pastor, my spiritual leader, so I held my peace. I watched my pastors use church funds for personal use. The first time it happened, my wife and I didn't know what to do. My wife and I taught a workshop that year, I was given a $350 honorary written from the church account. My wife was given a $650 check written from the church account, but it was NOT an honorary for her. It was made to look like an honorary, but it was not. She got nothing, but that was ok because my wife and I does not teach or preach for money. If we're given an honorary, we know how to receive it. We was told to cash that check for them *(my pastors)* and give the money to their son which was in college in North Carolina where we lived. They were funneling church money through us for personal use, trying to make it look legal, as though it was an honorary. Because we did not question their actions, they thought it was ok to do it again. The next time they mailed a $5500 Church check to my wife made payable to her and asked us to cash the check and go to the college and pay the first portion of their son's tuition, and against our better judgment we did it. But we talked about it this time and said what they are doing is not right and I need to say something to him *(my pastor)*, but my wife said no, just hold your peace, God sees what he is doing. Believe it or not he did it again. This time he sent a $7500 check written from the church account made payable to my wife and again asked us to cash it and go to the college and pay the rest of his sons' tuition. I told my wife, No! This is not right! Where is our integrity to let them fondle church money through us for personal use, I'm going to call him *(my pastor)* about this before you cash this check. I called my pastor and told him what you're doing is not right, you are miss using church funds for personal use. **Ephesians 4:28** says,*"Let him that stole steal no more: but rather let him labour, working with his hands the thing which is good, that he may have to give to him that needeth."* I said, don't ever send me or my wife another check written from the church account to cash and take care of personal business for you because we will not cash it! I said, pastor to do this, you don't really care about us, because what you're doing, you can get us in serious trouble with the Internal Revenue Service (IRS). He asked me, how is that going to get you in trouble? I said, pastor, you are making it look like you are paying us thousands of dollars for something that we have done, as it was an honorary, and we are not paying any taxes on that money. That's what it look like, and that can get us in trouble. He told me I can't get in any trouble because he is authorized to write these checks to whoever he wants to. I said to my pastor, yes you are authorized the write checks from the church account to take care of church business, but not to send to us to cash to take care of personal business for you. It's amazing how the devil can blind the mind of people no matter who you are, no matter what your title is, when it comes to money. I see why the scripture say, *"for the love of money is the root* *of all evil."* It makes you do things that you know is wrong but think that no one will ever find out about it. **Pastors, one thing for sure, people may forget what you say, <u>but people will never forget what you do</u>**. That's what the modern-day Pharisees do in this day and time, they sin and do things that is not right and hide it from the public eyes or put the blame on others.

Pastors, and church leaders, you have a responsibility and accountability to do the right thing with what God has put you over, and that's, people, and money, and not to abuse it.

Back to what I was saying about my pastor, again I told my pastor don't ever send me another check from the church account to cash and take care of personal business for you, because my wife and I will not cash it. My wife and I was not trusted very much after that, even though we did no wrong, we just stood for what was right, which we should have done the first time they asked us to cash a church check and take care of personal business for them. From that point, my pastor never sent me or my wife a church check ever again. Instead, when it was time to pay his son's college tuition, he would get on the airplane and fly here to North Carolina and have me to take him to the college and he would take care of business himself. What money he was using, church money or personal money, I don't know, and I have no idea, at that point it was none of my business, but I believe because of his character to do wrong, and try and justify it, he was still using church funds. Also, my pastor's other son, the youngest one went to college there locally with them, and I believe that he paid for his college tuition out of the church funds also. I have no proof of that, **I'm only going by my pastor's past character in this**. If a person's character shows a lack of integrity and use church funds to pay for one son's college tuition, I believe more than likely, he also paid for the other son's college tuition out of the church funds also. That son went to college locally right there with him, and my pastor had total control over the church funds. There was no oversight, no accountability, no one to answer to, no one to keep him on the straight and narrow, no one to see what he was doing. **Now, again, I have no proof of this, and I'm not saying he did it this way. I'm only going by my pastor's character in the past, and lack of integrity in this**. I believe if he did it for one son, he probably, I say again probably, did it for the other son also. One thing I know for sure, that the all-seeing eye of God sees everything, and if you don't own it and repent of it, the bible says, *"be sure your sin will find you out."* One thing for sure, no one gets away with what they have done forever, there will be a day of reckoning. God is long suffering, and have great mercy, and He's waiting on you to make it right, by owning your sins. God gives everyone the space to repent of their wrongness. Pride is what causes people not to own their wrongness, because they're trying to maintain a certain persona with others. Now, you might say why did I bring all this up? The reason I brought this up is because this book is about The Modern-Day Pharisees: The Uncovering, how religious leaders in this day and time are doing things in **secret, hidden, for personal gain**, and they are doing it in the name of the LORD, and these things need to be uncovered. Also, this book is about thirty-four years of ministry what you can learn from my experience. Jesus called those Pharisees in His day according to **Matthew 23:33** *"hypocrites, serpents, generation of vipers...,* and He also said to them, *...how can ye escape the damnation of hell?"* My pastors have done wrong, and will not own it, and there will be others. As pastors, I believe at some point, we all have done some kind of wrongness in our lives. The thing you must do when you do sin, is own it, by going to that person that you have wronged, and ask them to forgive you, and then go to God and confess it, and ask Him for forgiveness. If you don't feel as though you've done any wrong, you'll never go to that person that you have wronged, or own your wrongness, or confess it to God and ask for forgiveness. It's amazing how the devil has blinded the mind of those that believe. You are not the only one that has sinned as a pastor, and you won't be the last.

Listen to what happened in Goldsboro, North Carolina. Court document state, "pastor, charge with embezzlement. A local pastor is behind bars, and police says he stole more than $130,000 from his congregation. This pastor is accused of embezzlement from his church. Police said this pastor stole money and then, shut the church down and closed it. Police said the pastor even traded the church van for a personal vehicle for himself. Police says you hate to hear this kind of thing, you hate it for the people, who donated money to the church and the pastor took advantage of their trust." Again, this is how the modern-day Pharisee operate. They're all about themselves and don't care who they hurt in the process.

Listen to what happened in Stony Point, North Carolina. Court document state, "North Carolina Pastor, charged with insurance fraud. A pastor in Stony Point North Carolina was arrested and accused of taking about $23,000 in an insurance scam. Court document state, that AFLAC insurance company contacted the state department of insurance and said, this pastor, had filed a fraudulent disability claim while continuing to work full-time as the pastor, of his church."

Listen to what social media news reported that happened in Memphis, Tennessee: "several pastors, along with several business owners are indicted and charge with defrauding federal COVID-19 relief aid. This relief was supposed to help combat the worst pandemic in a century, but according to the department of justice, many of those charged was using the money to help themselves. The United States Department of Justice said these individuals, ranging from business owners to Memphis area church pastors, are charged in an almost million dollars in COVID-19 relief, fraud schemes. The federal grand jury return the indictments against the defendants for defrauding the disaster loan, and the paycheck protection program (PPP). The Justice Department said it's really cracking down on the defendants, charging them with various counts of wire fraud, illegally obtain $149,000 in relief aid each, they also received more than $150,000 in pandemic payments each, and almost $150,000 each in relief money. The Justice Department says the pastors lied on their applications and use the money for personal expenses. If convicted, they can face up to 20 years in federal prison on each fraud count." **Did you hear that, up to 20 years on <u>EACH</u> fraud count!**

This all comes down to greed! *"For the love of money is the root of all evil."* God didn't say money was evil, He said, for the love of it, meaning you'll do whatever it takes, legally or illegally to get it. That's how those that are not under anyone's leadership authority operate, there is no accountability, there is no oversight, so out of greed, they do whatever they want to do. Pastors and leaders, **<u>no one is above accountability and the law, even you!</u>**

Again, this is the modern-day Pharisees, how they do their deals for the love of money. The bible says, *"be sure your sin will find you out."* This is the action of pastors, that lack integrity, and it's not worth it. So, learn from these people example, don't do what they've done, you see what happened to them. Again pastors, as I said before, you are not the only one that has sinned or done wrong, and you won't be the last.

For the next five years my wife and I came to my pastor's church and was not asked to speak, or to teach, because we were not trusted very well, on what we might say. We were good with that, because we didn't care to speak or teach over there anyway. I think, I don't know for sure, but I think one reason they didn't ask us to speak, or teach is because, they were afraid that we would say something openly about what they were doing with church funds, so they walked on eggshells around us. We never said anything about it, to anyone. Neither did they, but they were always mindful when we were there at their church who we were talking to and about what.

My pastor had a young couple in their church that my wife and I had become very good friends with. The young lady father and I was stationed together at the same time in Okinawa Japan in the 80s while serving in the military. At that time, I think the young lady was only 10 or 12 years old, I don't remember. But the amazing thing is the next time I saw her was in another country, at my pastor church some years later. She and her husband, are now in their late twenty's, and in the military, and married. She didn't remember me, but I remembered her because I knew her dad very well. Her dad and I played football together while station in Okinawa, and she used to be on the sideline with his helmet on. To make a long story short, over the years, we all became very good friends, and my wife and I invited them to come to the states to North Carolina to spend a couple of weeks with us visiting. They accepted, so out of respect, we inform my pastor on our decision. My Pastors saw how close we had become and said that's not a good idea they don't need to come and visit with you guys for two weeks. I said why not, they're not in our ministry, they're in yours, and it's not a conflict of interest. My pastor's wife told me, that I am exactly right, they are in our ministry, and we have the say, and not me, and I don't think they should go, is not a good idea. I believe my pastors was in fear of what my wife and I might say to them while they are visiting with us, about what they have been doing with church funds, even though we wouldn't have. Readers! What are we reading about? We are reading about, The Modern-Day Pharisees: The Uncovering: how they do their deals in secret, and keep the things they've done hidden from the public eyes, and how they impose their will upon others to control them. So, they did not come for the visit, but we still remain friends to this day. They got out of the military, and was serving faithfully in my pastor's church for twenty years, and it had gotten to the point where they were not appreciated. They wanted to step away from my pastor's church for a little while for a break, and also to do some traveling, and my pastors was totally against it. If you've been in someone's ministry, supporting them 100% faithfully for twenty years, that person needs a break. So, feeling unappreciated, they left, and relocated to Texas, where they now live, and we thank God for their friendship, because they are genuine good people.

Through the years, I have watched people who have NOT proven themselves come into my pastor's ministry and get special treatment. They would get this special treatment over others who has been with him for years simply because of their high military rank, or special title. These people had not proven themselves in anyway, they just talked a good game. Their endgame was that when they needed something *(finances)*, they knew that they could get it from the pastor. They worked there deals to get money to do things in their ministry whenever it was needed. They never ever stood on their own two feet in faith, believing God that He would supply their every need. I know firsthand, because they would also call my wife and I and ask for money to financially support what they are doing. Pastors and church leaders, and future pastors and future leaders. When you have a leader that is needy, and you find yourself always supporting them, and always giving to them what ever they need, you are doing them an injustice. They will never grow spiritually, and mature to be able to stand in faith for themselves, because you're giving to them all the time. Example, that's like a child that's growing up learning how to walk, and every time that child falls down, dad is right behind that child holding them up, because he don't want to see the child fall. Falling for that child is part of learning how to walk on their own. After enough falls, that child learns to balance on their own two feet and walk. Another example, take that same child who is now grown up and become a teenager and you give them everything that they ask for. You never require them to work for it, or you never require them to figure things out for themselves, but you always stepping in, and giving that teenager everything they want. By bailing them out, and not allowing that teenager to figure somethings out for themselves, and when that teenager becomes an adult, you have done them a serious injustice. They now don't know how to do things for themselves. They don't know how to keep a job and make money for themselves. When things get tough on the job, they quit, because they don't know how to persevere. They don't know how to figure out problems for themselves. They don't know how to take care of, and pay their bills. They look for mom and dad to bail them out financially, and to figure out problems for them, and that's a serious injustice to them. They become nonproductive in society, and useless to the world. I know some parents personally who are ministers of the gospel, that hide and cover their own children's wrongness, but openly expose, and talk about other people, and their children's when they are wrong. Parents, you are also doing your children, a serious injustice when you cover and hide their wrongness, trying to make it look like they walk on water, and they are holier than thou, and they do, or have never done any wrongness. When people ask you how is Joey doing? And you say, Joey is doing fine, he's just doing fine, in all he do, God is really blessing him, when you know that's a lie. Joey won't go to college, he won't keep a job, he refused to obey you in your own home, you are constantly giving him finances when he asks for it, but yet you say he's doing fine. Now Joey hear you when you say this to others, and it makes him think, why do I need to change, because my parents are saying, I'm doing fine. Because *"faith comes by hearing"*, you are sowing the wrong thing into Joey's life, and he will say to himself my parents will cover, and hide my wrongness no matter what, and Joey will never change. He is one step from going to prison, but yet you are still covering and hiding his sins, and saying he's doing fine, and that's not helping him. Even so in ministry, when you have a spiritual leader, that have not learned to stand on their own two feet in faith, but they keep going to the spiritual parents, *(the pastors)*, every time there is a need, is wrong. Giving to them, or even paying for it for them, is a serious injustice. Pastors, you are not allowing that person to grow and mature in their faith as a spiritual leader. So, in return, they fail in ministry, and they have no members because of the accountability, and the responsibility, they have over the lives of others. God cannot afford to allow you to have His sheep, because you don't know how to shepherd them, and lead them by faith. How can you teach them to stand in faith, when you have never learned it yourself, when faith is the thing that pleases God. It's a disservice, and a dishonor to God's people, for you to shepherd them, and that's why you don't have any members. Now, let me go back to giving, don't get me wrong, I believe in sowing into good ground projects that other pastors are doing when I know it is a God-given vision. But when it's just a good idea, something you want to do just to make yourself look good, I can't support that. I can truly say in twenty-seven years of pastoring, my wife and I have never had to go to my pastor for any kind of financial support. Oh, trust me, I wanted to, many times! But I just kept hearing the Holy Spirit saying to me, stand in faith, believe God, stand in faith. My wife and I always stood on our own two feet, operating in faith, and God always came through for us.

Side Note: When I met my pastors in 1989, they were good young, genuine, leaders. His ministry was only three years old, small and still growing, they had genuine love and care for the people. They were good examples before the flock, and that's what drew me. I understand when you are growing physically, they're going to be growing pains, and some things have to change. Even so in ministry, as the ministry grows there are going to be growing pains, and some things have to change because of growth. If change is dictated, you change, but you don't stop loving or caring for the people and leading by example. Over the years as the membership grew to over 600 members, my pastors stop leading by example, and there were no more genuine love and caring for the people. It's like, they got beside themselves. It was all about them, and what they wanted. They were very abusive, talking to people any kind of way, in a very hateful way, like a drill sergeant, the way I used to talk to people in the early years of my ministry. Whatever they called right, it was right, whatever they called wrong it was wrong. If anyone questioned them about their actions on anything, my pastors would fabricate things and lie on that person, so that person would get upset, and leave the church, and they could continue to do their deals. This is how the Pharisees operated in Jesus times, and this is how the modern-day Pharisee operate in this day and time. They falsely accuse people, to get the focus off of themselves, and put it on others, so they can continue to do their deals. My wife and I would only be at their church for five days in January for the women's conference and four days in October for the men's conference. There's a lot of things that went on that we heard about through friends that was there, but the things that I am writing about in this book, my wife and I, saw them, and experienced them firsthand.

For 11 years I held my peace until March 2022, and I heard the Lord say now, **"SPEAK."** So, I tried to talk with my pastors, *(him and his wife)* on zoom, about not leading by example and other things that they were doing and not doing. This is the actual list of the things I emailed to them, while talking to them on zoom. I entitled it: **"What I need from my Leaders."**

First: I want to say I love you all. **Second**: I would like to say, I understand that you all are not perfect. **Third**: We are not going anywhere. We are standing on **Ecclesiastes 10:4 and 5** which says, *"If the spirit of the ruler rise up against thee, <u>leave not thy place</u>; for yielding pacifieth great offences. There is an evil which I have seen under the sun, as <u>an error which proceedeth from the ruler</u>:"*

1. I don't need to be bullied. Bullying only makes me stand up to the bully.
2. I need you to stop trying to change me. The only way you can change me is with love and kindness.
3. I need you to stop saying things about me that is not true. *(I told my pastors wife, you have said,*

I have said disrespectful things to pastor, and I get up and talk about things that you all don't teach.). I have never done such things.

4. I need you to stop holding things. *(April 2014).*

5. I need to hear I'm sorry, forgive me, I apologize when you are apologizing. *(I said it to my pastor's wife, on 3 June 2019 you said, "you needed to apologize to me for not being the leader you need to be to me for holding something against me", but you never apologized.)*

6. I need you to consider my feelings. *(I don't feel you do).*

7. I need you to stop looking for fault. Because when you look for fault, you will find fault. *(I need you to look for the good, and you will find it).*

8. I need you, when you see me say or do something wrong, I need you to do a proper critique or correction in a timely manner. *(not wait for weeks or months or even years to say something).*

9. I need you to lead by example. *(What you are doing and how you are acting, is that the example you want me to follow?)*

The big mistake I made was to email them this document while I was talking to them on zoom. My pastor's wife is a speed reader, and she read the entire document in a matter of a couple of minutes. She folded her arms, threw her head back, lean back in her chair and got mad. You could tell easily that she was mad, we were on zoom, and you could see her actions. That was my mistake I shouldn't have emailed the document to them; I should've just talked to them about these things. I told my pastors wife, she **bully** people, and it's not right for you to come down on people the way you do, that you feel as though they are beneath you. I said they are still God's people, and they should be treated and talk to with respect, love and kindness. I told her, she was miss using her authority, position and title, and I said, to my pastor, you are allowing it to happen. My pastor told me, I was talking to him like I was his pastor, when in fact, he is my pastor. I said no sir, I'm just pointing out what I see that is wrong, that needs to change. Pastor when a person cannot see their own wrongness, and how they are treating others, someone has to be man or woman enough, and willing to stand up, and speak up, as I am doing right now. God is not going to speak out of the sky to correct wrongness. He has to have a willing vessel, someone that is full of faith and has integrity that is willing to stand for what is right, that he can work and speak through. As I stated earlier, we should tell each other the truth when we see each doing wrong, and don't lie to each other, trying to maintain favor. If the truth can't keep us together, then just maybe, we don't need to be together. I said pastor, you are requiring us to do certain things that you're not doing yourself, and that's not leading by example. You require us to give 10% of our tithes and offering that comes into our church each month to your church, which is tithe the tithes, and we understand that. We have done that faithfully without fail, for twenty-two years, and we have no problem with doing that. The problem I have, is you don't do it yourself, because you're not under anyone's authority to be accountable to, you have no pastor over you, and have NEVER had a pastor over you to answer to. So, you are requiring us to do what you're not doing, and you and your church gives to no one. Also, you require us to give financial gifts of love to you and your wife personally every month. My wife and I, not our church, have been giving financial gifts of love to you and your wife for twenty-two years faithfully each month without fail. I asked my pastors, when have you ever given anything to my wife and I? My wife and I have been pastoring under you for twenty-five years, and we can only recount only two times that you gave a love offering gift to us, and we can only recount two times you given to our church, and that's not leading by example. **Only two times in twenty-five years that's all you have given**, and my wife and I and our church has given to you and your church every month for twenty-two years. I reminded my pastor, how we gave just in the four years and nine months of doing the building of the new church, my wife and I, personally gave unto you and your wife, not your church, but you personally, $40,725. And my church gave to your church, $72,000. The grand total of giving to you and your church, was $112,725 total, doing the four years and nine months of building of our new church building, **and that was just four years and nine months of giving**. My pastor's wife said to me, "so what, what's your point?" You mean after all that I have just said to you, all you can ask me is **<u>what's my point</u>**! Wow! If you can't realize in all that I have just said, that you're not leading by example then there's nothing else for me to say. My pastor's wife said, whenever you all asked us for any kind of financial help we have always sent it to you. I said that's not true, because we have never ever asked you all for any financial help in twenty-five years of ministry. My wife and I have always stood on our own two feet in faith, and believe God for whatever we needed. I said to my pastor's wife, what does that have to do with what I am talking to you all about, **NOT leading by example? She said, "you don't have the right to talk to us about that, or to point out our wrongness."** I said why NOT, everyone has some wrongness, including you, and it's what I and others see. I'm just the only one that is bold enough to talk to you about these things, and not talk behind your back, like others are doing! And that's where the problem lyes with my pastors, thinking that they are above the law, and don't have to follow laws, rules or guidelines, because they are not accountable to anyone. Readers, what are we reading about in this book? We are reading about The Modern-Day Pharisees: The Uncovering, how they silence the people, how it's all about you doing what they want you to do, and not question it. How it's all about how they impose their will upon others to get all they can out of you, it's all about themselves. Unfortunately, what I had to say fell on deaf ears, and was NOT received at all, because they believe they have done no wrong. I understand that no one wants to hear about their wrongness, or not doing what they should be doing, it's all right to hear about someone else's, but not mine!

That's what I am talking about in this book, The Modern-Day Pharisees: The Uncovering, how they do their deals in secret, and they can't receive correction, believing they are never wrong.

Listen to what Jesus says in **Luke 7:30** *"But the Pharisees and lawyers rejected the counsel of God against themselves... ."* Notice how the Pharisees rejected wise counsel that Jesus gave them, against themselves, believing that they've done no wrong. The same thing still goes on today, with pastors, and leaders, rejecting council from others, believing they've done no wrong.

Of course, in the early years of my ministry I did not want to hear about my wrongness either, when someone pulled me to the side and talk to me about mine. But thank God, I had enough common sense, and spiritual insight, to listen, and I received it, because it changed my life and my ministry for the better. Pastors, and church leaders, God is not going to speak out of the sky and tell you, you are wrong, He is going to use someone to tell you. When God use someone to tell you about your wrongness, they are telling you for your own good, you just have to have an ear to hear and a heart to receive.

I don't remember what year it was, but one year my wife and I came to one of the conferences, and after the conference was over, we stayed over for a day or two visiting. We were invited to the pastor's house for fellowship. To make a long story short, while in the house we began to look at the different pictures and certificates on the wall. I noticed my pastor's ordination, that he was ordained by his wife's first cousin *(I won't call his name)*. I inquired about the ordination and his wife started explaining. When I was in college working on my doctorate in counseling, one thing I learned is to let the person talk. In this case I did, and she told it all. She told us when her husband was in the military station at Fort Gordon, in Augusta Georgia, he attended a church there for the time he was there. But when it was time for the military to move him, they sent him overseas to another country, but before he left, that pastor DID NOT ordain him. She said when he got overseas, he fellowshipped with other pastors at different churches. She said, in 1986 he was led to start his own ministry, so he did, but was NOT ORDAINED. When he tried to minister in the chapel on the military installation, he was told by the chaplain he could not because he was NOT ORDAINED. Now, you might say why am I bringing this up this way? It plays a very important role in what I was told when I first met my pastor, in 1989. **The things that I was told was untrue!** He told me that he was ordained by the pastor in Augusta Georgia, and that was not true, that was a lie. I told him I also know the pastor there, because I also attended that church for a while when I were stationed there in 1991. Again, I don't remember what year it was that we stayed over for a couple of extra days visiting. But after talking to my pastor about the ordination on his wall, I asked him why you don't acknowledge this guy that ordained you as your pastor? He answered, **"that's just my wife first cousin."** I said, you know, whoever ordained you, for whatever reason, that person is your pastor, whether you want them to be or not, and whatever spirit is upon them, is also upon you. From that day to this, my pastor, would always tell people that his pastor *(the pastor in Augusta Georgia)* died. Well, that's sort of true, but it's not the whole truth. After he *(the pastor, in Augusta Georgia)* being found out, that he had embezzle over $2 million from his church and was being brought up on charges, he committed suicide. I said all of that, to say this, a lot of pastors out their ministry is founded and built on untruths, and their sins has been covered for years. As long as your sins are covered, and hidden, you will never prosper in ministry the way God intended for you to prosper, because it sends the wrong message to you. It is saying to you, God is allowing me to prosper, so why not continue doing the things that I am doing, and just continue to hide it, and look, I am still successful. **Proverbs 28:13** says, *"He that covereth* (hide) *his sins shall not prosper... ."* You might have a certain level of success in ministry, but never on the level that God intended, because of your hidden sins. These are the things that the Pharisees did in Jesus' time they covered their sins and lies but exposed the sins that others did to make themselves look good and holy. You can see in this, that the modern-day Pharisee are doing the same thing in this day and time, and it has to be exposed. **Numbers 32:23** says, *"...behold, ye have sinned against the Lord: and be sure your sin will find you out."* My pastor has always led people to believe that he was ordained under the pastor in Augusta Georgia, and he still says it to this day, **"my pastor died,"** and that's a lie. For thirty-seven years as a pastor, he has never had to answer to anyone, and still to this day answer to no one. Wow! He has never been under anyone's authority, there has never been any oversight, no accountability, no one to answer to, no one to keep him on the straight and narrow, and for thirty-seven years he have had absolute power to do whatever he want to.

Now, let me stop here, and talk to you about the danger of absolute power. Absolute power will always lead to absolute abuse and corruption. If you are a leader and especially a church leader that has no oversight, or no accountability, meaning you have no one to answer to or no one to keep you honest and on the straight and narrow, you will abuse your position, title, money, and people. If you have no oversight over you or you refuse to submit to the oversight that is over you, you are headed for a fall and great shall be your fall! Every pastor should be under someone's authority, if not, you can very easily get yourself into serious trouble. I've heard some pastors that's not under anyone's authority say, I am under the authority of the Holy Spirit. That's foolishness, and that's not bible, and that's not God, that's a bunch of junk. No one wants to hear that kind of foolishness, because every pastor should be under someone's authority, someone to answer to. **Hebrews 13:17** says, *"Obey them that have the rule over you, and submit yourselves: for they watch for your souls, as they that must give account, that they may do it with joy, and not with grief: for that is unprofitable for you."* Notice what this verse says, *"obey them to have rule over you and submit,"* this is very clear, there is no misunderstanding this. God says two things here; number one He said **"obey"** which means *to do or carry out what* *someone says*. Number two He said **"submit"** which means **to *accept or yield to a superior force, or to the authority or will of another person***. This verse tells me that IF, and that is a BIG IF, you are truly call by God, we all must be under someone's authority, someone to submit to, someone to answer to, someone to help keep us on the straight and narrow. It's the same principal that God talks about in **Proverbs 29:15** where he says, *"...a child left to himself bringeth his mother to shame."* It's the same principal with a pastor that is not under anyone's authority, if he is left to himself, he shall bring his ministry, and himself to an open shame, by abusing his or her authority. What are we reading about in this book? We are reading about, the modern-day Pharisee, who does not submit to anyone's authority, but go about establishing their own righteousness. A pastor that is not under someone's authority, is one that goes about establishing his or her own righteousness. He or she is calling right wrong and wrong right, and don't know the difference and that is dangerous, and you are headed for a fall.

Over the years I watch my pastor's ministry grow from a small ministry to over 600 members. But I also watched it go down to where it is today, just a hand full of people, compare to what he had, because of hidden sins, and ineffective communication, and leadership skills. People don't just leave your ministry for no reason; people leave a ministry for all kinds of reasons to include a lack of good leadership, and pastors that should not be so. We should always strive to be better leaders, you never get to the point where you have arrived, meaning you are all knowing when it comes to leadership. People should never be leaving your ministry because you lack the ability to lead them. Pastors everything begins and ends with us, success, or failure. On Sunday mornings my pastor's wife would say, where are the people, I don't understand why they are not coming? When you are operating in sin, God can't even allow you to even have the appearance that you're successful, because it sends the wrong message to you, and that's why the people are not coming or has left. A lot of times when people leave a ministry is because God has truly laid on their heart to leave that ministry because of the hidden sins, of the pastor. The problem that I see with my pastors is, they lack empathy and compassion, and a lack of education, and because of a lack of these things they don't know how to communicate effectively with others, so they bully people instead. Leaders and future leaders, educate yourself and learn to have compassion, and empathy, with others when you are talking to them, or when they are talking to you about a matter. Learn to view things from that person's point of view. It doesn't mean that you're wrong, or that they are right, **it's just a different view**, because you are not always the smartest person in the room. There's always someone else that knows a little bit more than you do. I know you want to be the smartest person there, but you can't always have your way. College education is a help, the Holy Spirit can enhance that education, and it will help you be successful in ministry, and it helps you to be successful in all that you do. **Now,**

please don't get me wrong, you don't have to have a college degree to preach the gospel, because the Holy Spirit can show you how to do things beyond your education. But that is not true in all cases, because you can see in a lot of pastor's actions, they needed a college education to help them make better decisions. My pastor was in the military for twenty years, but the highest rank he ever earned, was Sergeant E5 promotable, which is the lowest Non-Commission Officer *(NCO)* rank, in the Army, and there is a lot of wrong things with that. That's someone that did not pursue higher education or did not push themselves to be better, or just lack the motivation or self will to pursued other things that would help them get promoted and be successful in his career. Twenty years in the military, but never excelled in his career, and that's why you never ever hear him talk about his military career. His wife was also in the military, but for only twelve years, and she pushed herself and earned the rank up to Staff Sergeant/E6, which was very good. But because she could not control herself, after being told several times verbally, and in writing, to stop doing certain things, she just figured the rules didn't apply to her, and she kept doing those things. So, she was punished, and demoted and reduced back down to the rank of Sergeant/E5, and that's a shame because of a lack of self-control. You might look at this and say, well! Where did they get their leadership training from for ministry if they only earned the rank of Sergeant/E5 in the military and only have a high school education? Again, don't get me wrong. I believe that the Holy Spirit can guide you in direct you how to do things in ministry without a college education, and you will be very successful at it. But like I said earlier, that might not be in all cases, in every ministry, or with every person **because of the condition of the person's heart**. The Holy Spirit cannot lead you, or guide you into all truth if you have hidden sin. As I stated before, my pastors have never set under anyone that they had to answer to, or give an account to, or to report to, so they don't really understand what leadership is. They just make it up as they go, and call it leadership. I should know, I served twenty-two years in the military as I stated earlier and retired at a rank of Sergeant First Class/E7. I pushed myself to be all I could be as an NCO, and I was rewarded with promotions. I attended, and completed all of the advance leadership courses that was offered and required for a Sergeant First Class/E7 or above. My last three assignments, I served as a First Sergeant/E8, that's a pay grade a step above what I currently am, and I led over 425 soldiers in my company. Now, I am not trying to toot my own horn, and I am not bragging, and it is not pride. One might say, why did you bring up your military career, while talking about your pastor and his wife military career? The only reason why is this, anyone reading this could see that I should know what I'm talking about because of my higher rank, leadership training, and twenty-two years of military service. I am proud that I had the opportunity to serve in the military for twenty-two years, and received some of the best leadership training in the world. This training has definitely been a big help in ministry, and no one can ever take the training from me. Anyone that has served for twenty years or more and obtain the rank of Sergeant First Class/E7 or higher, knows that a person that spends twenty years in the military, and only obtain the rank of Sergeant/E5 promotable could only go but so far as a leader. That's not the characteristics of a good leader, because they themselves in twenty years, has never pushed themselves to be better. So how can they push someone else to be better, or to lead someone else? They can't! According to U.S. Army doctrine, as a NCO the eleven principles of leadership is what guides us as an effective leader. Principal **number one** says: **"Know yourself and seek self-improvement:"** *To know yourself* is to understand who you are, your values, priorities, your strengths and weaknesses. ***Self-improvement*** is to always seek new ways to improve yourself, like education, because **knowledge is power**. Principal **number two** says: **"Be technically and tactically proficient:"** Before a leader can lead effectively, they must first master the tasks that they require of others. How can you tell someone else how to do something, when you can't do it yourself. These two principles along tells you that you must do all that you can do to be better, so you can lead others by example. How can you tell someone else to do something when you can't even do it yourself? A good leader leads by example in every way. Now, who serves in the military for twenty years and retire at the rank of E5? I'll tell you who, someone who never pushed themselves to be better, or someone who always stayed in trouble. Now, I'm not saying he's someone that always stayed in trouble, I'm just saying from my twenty-two year experience in the military, and retiring as a Sergeant First Class (SFC/E7) it has to be one of these two things. My pastor and I join the military the same year, 1976. He can't use the excuse, saying that I was in one of those MOS's (Military Occupational Skills), that had a high cut off promotion score, so was I, and that's no excuse. Anyone that join the military in the 70s was in one of those MOS's that had a high cut off promotion score, you had to do more then sitting back doing nothing, to reach the cut off score, so you could get promoted. You had to take advantage of schools and courses that the military offered free of charge, and I did, so I got promoted. A lot of people sit back on the stool of do nothing for twenty years, and that's why they didn't advance in their career, and that was no one's fault but their own. To be successful in what you are doing, it requires something of you, but if you don't do what is required of you, then you will fail, and that's on you. By the way, let me say this about my wife, she also served in the military for eight years, and in those short eight years she had earned the rank of Sergeant/E5 promotable which was very good. She was an instructor who taught classes to the other soldiers. As her husband, I made sure that my wife was a great leader as a Sergeant/E5 promotable, she was a super trooper. She had gotten approved to attend Drill Sergeant School, when she was involved in a automobile accident, and had a severe shoulder injury and could no longer do push-ups, and made a decision to get out of the military on a medical discharge. That's the only reason why I brought up our careers, we both was well trained. It's the favor of God, on us, it's just proof through our military training and being led and guided by the Holy Spirit, that we understand leadership, and effective communication.

When trying to talk with my pastors, it is always a monologue with them, and never a dialogue. You are told to just stop talking, and listen, but never given the opportunity to talk. You never get the opportunity to complete a statement before you are cut off, and they would say things like, nobody wants to hear what you have to say because all you do is lie. Now, who is going to stay under that type of leadership, no one! To be a leader, that is a narcissistic leadership style, and it is not good, and it has no place in ministry or any organization. Pastors, God see what you're doing, and also doing in secret, and he can't allow your ministry to be successful or to prosper. These are the things that the Pharisees did in Jesus' time, they silence the people, and these are the things that the modern-day Pharisee are doing in this day and time, and it need to be exposed, and it need to stop. That is why the Holy Spirit has led me to write this book, The Modern-Day Pharisees: The Uncovering. The Pharisees is all about themselves. It's about they themselves being seen and being heard and no one else. Jesus talked about how they would pray on the street corners with long prayers just to be heard and seen of men, having the form of godliness but far from it. Jesus said they have their reward. Jesus was saying, they have no reward of My Father in heaven their reward was just what they got, to be heard and seen of men. I believe one of the worst things you can do as a pastor or leader, is to pretend that you're something that you're not. I have watched my pastor over the years visit different churches to try and get in good with the pastor so the pastor of that church would invite him back to be a guest speaker. Wherever he *(my pastor)* goes, he always expects to speak. Now granite, whenever my pastor, come to North Carolina to my church I have always given him the honor position to be the speaker. That is the right thing to do. That's not a bad thing, but it becomes a bad thing when you are not given that honor position to be the speaker and you then, get mad, and get bent all out of shape about it. You have now entered into pride. What a shame, thinking you're all of that, and God can only use you. Shame on you to think that way. Jesus said in **Matthew 12:34**, *"out of the abundance of the heart the mouth speaketh."* Oops, there it is, and that means it's a condition of your heart.

Let me tell you what my pastor did to me in 2016 that was very inconsiderate, but I don't hold it against him. You might say, why are you bringing it up, if you don't hold it against him. The reason why, is because everyone has some wrongness, and it's so that you the readers might learn from another person's mistakes, and it's because of what I am talking about in this book, The Modern-Day Pharisees: The Uncovering, how is all about themselves, how they impose, or force their will upon others. He came to the states to take care of some personal business. He flew into Greenville

North Carolina, to his sister's house. It's about a two in a half hour drive from Fayetteville North Carolina where I live, and where he was coming to take care of personal business. He could've flown direct to Fayetteville, but instead he wanted to go visit his sister first, that's why he flew into Greenville. I totally understand that, and I have no problem with that. The problem I have is when you're so selfish, and self-righteous, you don't consider others. I'm a commercial pilot and have been flying for over twenty years and have thousands of flight hours. I bought my wife and I a personal airplane back in 2015, also with my pastor in mind, so whenever he come to the states, I don't have to do a lot of driving to go pick him up, or driving him to Atlanta Georgia, I can just fly him, and save a lot of time, because I really hate driving. Now my wife and I bought this airplane so we can do some traveling, it's part of our retired life, God has blessed us greatly. I'm not bragging, just giving a good report. We didn't buy a small crop duster, but we bought a top-of-the-line small personal airplane; it's called a Cirrus SR20. Google it and look it up so you can see what it look like. It's one of the best and safest small personal planes on the market today. To save time, I could fly up and pick him up, and bring him back to Fayetteville, which is only a 35-minute flight there, and a 40-minute flight back. Round-trip an hour and twenty-five minutes. To drive up to pick him up, would be a two-and a half-hour drive to Greenville, and a two-and a half-hour drive back to Fayetteville, five hours round-trip, depending on the traffic, and the rest of my day is shot. When he flew in, and call me to come pick him up, I told him I would fly up and pick him up. He said, "oh no oh no, I'm not flying". The reason I said Google my Cirrus SR20 and look it up, is because I want you to see that is not something that you would be afraid to fly in. The airplane has a built-in parachute, and if there's a problem, you pull the parachute, and the entire airplane comes down on the parachute, there is no jumping out. Like I said, it's one of the safest, personal airplanes on the market today. I said you can't be afraid to fly, you just got off of an airline flying ten hours. He said, "no, I'm not afraid, I'm just not going to fly". I said, I know you not afraid to fly with me, because you flown with me years ago, right after I got my pilots license, and at that time I had less than 100 hours of flight time, now that would've been the time to be afraid. He said, "I'm not afraid, just drive up and pick me up". Now, isn't that very inconsiderate, and doesn't that sound just like the modern-day Pharisees, just what I am talking about in this book. No consideration for others, they are all about themselves, they impose their will and desires on others to accomplish their purpose, and doesn't care how it inconvenience others. I said yes sir pastor, I will be there. Pastors and leaders don't do this to your people, they actually have a life. To make a long story short I drove up to Greenville and picked him up, brought him back to Fayetteville, a total of five hours round-trip, what a waste of time. But what are we reading about in this book, The Modern-Day Pharisees: The Uncovering, how they impose their will upon others and is all about themselves. Pastors and church leaders, you should always be considerate of those that are around you, those that are serving in the ministry, and not take advantage of them, and abuse them. Now, in my old life, before I got saved, back in early 1989, I would've told my pastor where he could go, and you can find your own way to Fayetteville. But thank God the old me is dead, and I'm saved, sanctified, and filled with the Holy Ghost, and know how to be honorable and respectful.

Ok, going back to March 2022, what I was talking about earlier, before I ventured off on this side note about my pastors. I tried to talk with my pastors, *(him and his wife)* about not leading by example and other things. I told my pastor's wife, you **"bully"** people, trying to get them to do what you want them to do, and that's not how it's done, and that's not right, and that's not leadership. Pastors and future leaders don't be like that, you have got to learn to use empathy, and compassion when you're dealing with people, no matter who they are, and no matter what they have done. What I had to say to them was not received at all. Instead, for the next two years they came after my wife and I with vengeance, trying to run us out the ministry, so the things that we knew about them, that they had done and it's probably still doing, doesn't get out, but we refuse to leave. Remember, I've been with my pastor for thirty-four years faithfully and have done everything that is asked of me. I heard the Lord say to me stand firm and stay put, and to meditate on **Ecclesiastes 10:4-5** that says, *"If the spirit of the ruler rise up against thee, **leave not thy place**; for yielding pacifieth great offences. There is an evil which I have seen under the sun, as **an error***

which proceedeth from the ruler*.*" So, you can see in these scriptures, God is telling you when you go through something, stand firm, and don't be moved, because sometimes even the ruler, *(pastor)*, is wrong. <u>Pastors, there's no one around you that is perfect</u>, **including you**, so learn how to be compassionate. After those two years, my pastor and his wife saw, that my wife and I was not going to leave them on our own, so something else had to be done. One thing I've learned in thirty-four years, is, you have to know when to leave a ministry or when to stay put, because, just maybe, God has not finished with you yet. What happened to you was just a stumble in your walk with the Lord, or just a bump in the road, but don't let that be the end of your journey, because God's purpose has to be fulfilled. No one should ever be defined by one or two bad decision they made in life but be given a second chance to land on their feet, to shine, and prove who they really are. **Proverbs 27:17** says, *"Iron sharpeneth iron; so a man sharpeneth the countenance of his friend."* That means we should all make each other better, and not worse, by holding things against each other that we have done. God is always looking for someone that has integrity and is full of faith that he can work through to accomplish his purpose.

Side note, I believe this will help you pastors, and future pastors that are reading this book. When people leave your ministry for whatever reason, either something you've done or said, or something they have done, let them go. Do not run behind people that has left your ministry trying to get them to come back. They will never come back to your church and for goodness' sake, don't talk about those that has left, but pray for them. For whatever reason they left, you can't change that. Don't focus on them at all, let them go, because they will never come back, only focus on the people that are still with you. I don't understand why when people cut ties with you, and leave your church, they want to see you fail. My pastors wanted to see my wife and I fail, because they weren't the guest speaker at our new church grand opening service, so they thought, and that's a shame. But the sad thing is, for pastors to go so far to tell those people when you leave, or because you left their church, your marriage going to fall apart, you are going to lose your job, you're going to lose all your money, you're going to be in debt, your church is going to shut down. They just speak a lot of gloom and doom over people when they leave the church. To do that pastor, is very poor leadership, and it ought not to be. Pastor and future leaders, a true leader will never do that, when people go their separate way, a true leader will wish you well.

Now, you know just because you have the option to leave a ministry, doesn't mean you should leave. Sometimes the door is open, but God doesn't want you to leave yet. Remember the story in the book of Acts the 16th chapter, it says that Paul and Silas were beaten, put in chains and thrown into the inner part of the prison, that means in the dungeon, the bottom of the prison, where the rats, the sewage, dark and smelly, the worst part of the prison. It says at midnight they begin to sing praises unto God. The bible says when they do, the prison began to shake, and the chains fell off of them, and everyone in the prison, and the doors of the prison swung open. The keeper of the prison *(prison guard)* came in, and he saw the doors open, he assumed that the prisoners had escaped. So, he took out his sword to kill himself, because everyone had escaped, and that meant death for him for letting them escape. But Paul cried out, and said to him, *"do yourself no harm, we are all here."* The keeper of the prison came and fell down before Paul and said, what must I do to be saved? **That man in his whole household gets saved, because Paul stayed**. The power of this story is not that God open the doors, or the chains falling off, but the power of this story is, that Paul was spiritual enough to know that his assignment had not been completed, so he couldn't leave, even though he was in a bad situation. Some of us, we just want to get out of the bad situation, and want the problems to end, and we don't know the assignment for the problem yet. It's not until you have the option to leave sometimes, and then God revealed why you were in it in the first place. Paul and Silas were beaten, and put in prison to save a man, and his family. Maybe you went through what you went through are going through, to save someone else, or to be God's mouthpiece. Now! are you too selfish to stay put, and let God complete his purpose through you? Are you too concerned about your freedom that you don't care about the will of God being accomplished. There's something more to your pain than what you went through, to just give up, and leave. That's a terrible life to live. I refuse to believe that God allows me to go through purposeless pain. There's something in this, and I have to have the wisdom and discernment, to stay until the purpose is revealed, or when to actually leave. Even though God has caused the change to fall off of them, and open the doors to the prison, they could've left at any time, but I'm sure Paul said to himself, there has to be a purpose for me being in this dungeon. The doors are open, but I can't just leave, there has to be another reason. **When the prison guard fell at Paul's feet, and said,** *"what must I do to be saved."* **I'm sure Paul said, ok, this is why I'm here!** God's purpose was revealed to Paul at that time, but if he had left, the purpose of being there, would have never been revealed to him, and the man and his household would have never gotten saved. We just have to be willing and obedience to stay put until God's purpose has been revealed to us.

Pastors and church leaders don't allow yourselves to become so religious or spiritual, or so self-righteous till you're no earthly good. Meaning, people don't want to be around you or hear what you have to say or talk about because of your holier than thou attitude. They know all you are going to do is quote a lot of scriptures at them. First, you need to show them that you are approachable, by smiling and talking with them about other things, it shows them that you are human just as they are. Sometime when you are talking to others you need to talk to them plainly, and come down on their level, right where they are, just as Jesus did, and they will be ready to listen, and receive what you have to say.

Back to my pastors, since my wife and I refuse to leave on our own, **we were told by our pastors on July 3, 2023, we will not be your pastors any longer. We are releasing you both from the ministry, they said go get under someone else, and let them be your pastor.** What more can we say! There is nothing more we can say, because they are the ones in charge. I said, so after thirty-four years this is how you are going to end this relationship? They said yes! I could only imagine what my pastor's wife has fabricated on us to others, the reason why we left, but you know what, who cares! All we could say is OK. Honestly, we were GOOD with it. It was liberty for us. It felt as though great weights were lifted off of us. We believe that God had completed and accomplished His purpose for us being under them for thirty-four years. Maybe it was to tell them, I don't know, how wrong they've been in different things, because no one else would stay put long enough for God to use them. Or maybe it was to write this book. All I know, <u>in our spirits, there was a calm and a piece that came over us</u> **when they released us.** It was a joy, unspeakable, and full of glory. It was a joy and peace that surpassed all understanding. It was a joy and piece that the human finite mind could not comprehend. We were free! We had freedom from all the tyranny, and lying, and false accusations and deliberate misleading statements to others about us, by our pastors. My wife and I understand, that some relationships is for a reason, and some relationships is for a season, and some relationships is for a lifetime. But every relationship has a start time, and an end, it has a reason for you being there, and yet there are others that is only for a season, and that's to accomplish God's purpose. But still there are relationships for a lifetime, such as a marriage, or your connection to Jesus Christ, where you are forever growing by being connected to that person. You should ask yourself this question, what kind of relationship am I connected to? Relationship is a connection between persons by blood, marriage, spiritually, or emotionally. As Christians, we are connected to God through the blood of Jesus Christ. **Hebrews 9:12** says, *"Neither by the blood of goats and calves, but by his own blood he entered in once into the holy place, having obtained eternal redemption for us."* It's very important that you understand how God connects us to others through relationship, and why you are connected. Relationship connections flow in one of three ways. **1. a Season,** *(a little while, or temporary)*, **2. a Reason,** *(something God has for you through someone else)*, and **3. a Lifetime,** *(you are forever growing through that connection in ways only God knows and He will reveal it to you later along your course of destiny)*. However you are connected ***(season, reason or lifetime)***, you must ask yourself the question; was that relationship put here by God, or was it put here by the enemy? The enemy put some relationships in your life to get you off the course that God has prepared for you. So ask yourself this question also; why am I connected to whom I am connected to? When something doesn't go your way ***(yes I said it, your way)***, God is not necessarily telling you to leave the relationship, that might just be growth. Knowing the relationship and why you are connected to it is very important for your success. I challenge you to be different, stop running and stay connected! I truly believe in this ordeal that my wife and I have gone through for these last two years, God was showing us that this relationship is over. One thing I do know is this, God put people in your life for a reason, and when that reason is completed, He will remove them from your life, and establish a new relationship with someone else, for a better reason, because no one person is all knowing, or have it all together. God will allow one door to close in your life, and open another to complete His purpose. We're just excited about the next part of the planned of God for our ministry, and our lives.

Leaders, people might not ever know anything about what you have done, or been doing, or even still doing, but remember, God sees, and knows all things.

I heard the Lord say to me, with a loud voice, you've been loyal and faithful to your pastor for thirty-four years. **"NOW WRITE!"**

From this point, I can't call him my pastor any longer, **<u>because he released us</u>**, so I will use the term for the rest of this book **"my former pastor."** I believe the real reason that my former pastor release my wife and I from under them, is because we knew things about them that they had done that could get them in serious trouble. And also twice my former pastor asked me to host a men's conference for him, and I didn't do it. But the reason why, in February 2023 my wife and I had just gotten over Covid-19 when he wanted me to host one for him, but we were still in recovery from Covid. That's why I didn't want to do it the first time he asked, and I explained that. The second time he asked was in May 2023, but I had already planned and was hosting my own men's conference, and I believe my former pastor wanted me to cancel my men's conference to hold a men's conference for him and I wouldn't do it. Pastors, and future pastors, never cancer what God has told you to do, to do something for someone else no matter who it is. It's not a lack of honor, a respect, but it's you doing what God told you to do. When God tells you to do something, God is trying to take you someplace higher. So I told my former pastor, I mean no disrespect, but I just don't have time, I have a lot going on. I told him, let me explain to you everything I have going on this year, but he didn't want to hear it, he told me, no, I don't have to explain anything to him. If I don't want to do it just don't do it. He was just coming my way and he thought that he just hold the men's conference at my church since he was coming my way.

That was just a copout, he was really just testing the water to see would I do it. Just like he did for their church anniversary service, they invited my wife and I to be there, but unfortunately, we didn't realize that our passports had expired during the pandemic. So we told them we couldn't come because of that, so in that, they couldn't get a true feel of the test of our hearts towards them. Now my former pastor couldn't come this way and support us on our new church building dedication grand opening service, but you can come this way so I can host a men's conference for you. The Holy Spirit said to me, he is really just testing you to see if you would hold a men conference for him, since he didn't come support you and your wife on your new church grand opening building dedication service. I whole nothing against my former pastors, I just didn't have time at that time. I explained to him, I can do it at another time as long as it doesn't conflict with something that I have already planned, but he didn't want to hear it. He told me again, you don't have to explain, I was just coming your way at that time, if you don't want to do it, just don't do it. My former pastor, and anyone that's reading this book know he was wrong, for not coming and supporting me and my wife on our new building dedication service, but he don't know how to apologize for that. Again, that's OK, because my wife and I hold nothing against them. His heart is so hard towards me and my wife, because I would not cancel what I was doing, and do what he wanted me to do for him at that time, and that's a shame. Let me show you what I mean about the condition of his heart. I sent him a message on Facebook messenger, as I have done in the past, requesting to purchase twenty of his books that I talked about in chapter four, to sell in our bookstore, and **he would not sale them to me, he would not even reply**. I don't understand, how a person can claim to be so spiritual, but yet deprive the people from the information that is presented in his book, because it's really a good book. God knows what is in a person's heart, and He can't allow us to even have the appearance that we are successful in anything that we do, when our heart is not right. God knows the heart of everyone, even though we don't know what that person hidden motive is.

Chapter 7: The Narcissistic Leader

Let me take the time and talk about the narcissistic leader, and their style of leadership. Do you know what a narcissistic leader is? A narcissistic leader is a person who has an excessive interest in or admiration of themselves, one's physical appearance, selfish, a lack of empathy, very controlling, very condescending, has a bully style leadership, when angry very defensive, very manipulative, will not listen to others, they desire to be admired, and they have an excessive desire to win the notice of others, because it's all about themselves, and no one else. The narcissistic leader becomes very hostile when challenged, they are very quick to criticize others, because they feel as though they have done no wrong. They feel as though others can be wrong, but not them, and they fail to see anything wrong in what they do. When they are wrong, and it comes up in the conversation, they will always deflect, to get the attention off of themselves. The narcissistic leader feed off of people that are men pleasers, or people pleasers, they will recruit those that are less confident in themselves and is more loyal, they need you, to need them, that's how they exist. The narcissistic leader is in it solely for his or her own enrichment, it's all about themselves, and they will steal from the church, or organization whenever they have the opportunity to do so, because it's all about their enrichment. The narcissistic leader will come off as having a special connection with God that others do not have, God can only use them. If you say, God told me to do dus-in-so, they will say God never told you any such thing, because they thank God can only use them, and no one else. A narcissistic leader carries him or herself in this way; no matter how hard you work or how good you do a job, or how good your idea were, it's never good enough for them. It will **ALWAYS** be, you did great, **BUT** I believe you can do better. The reason why they do this is, they see greatness in you, but it's all about themselves being great and not you. They will put you down, and say your work was not good enough, and that is because they will steal your work or ideals for themselves, and present it as their own. **Now don't get me wrong, I'm not talking about constructive criticism, which is use to grow and to mature a person, to point out what they did wrong, so they can improve to be better.** I am talking about a narcissistic leader, that will try and make you feel worthless, who will exploit your weaknesses for their own gain, because is all about themselves. The narcissistic leader will ask you to do unethical things that make you feel very uncomfortable to do, like my former pastors did my wife and I, to cash church checks for them, and go and pay their son's college tuition for them. The narcissistic leader will abuse their authority, and they will find a way to justify what they have asked you to do. They will start by asking you to do little things, and then eventually they will ask you to do bigger things. **Song of Solomon 2:15** says, *"...the little foxes, that spoil the vines... ."* It's the little things that we do that we don't give attention to, that eventually turns into big things, and get totally out of control. If you do that thing that they asked you to do that is unethical the first time no matter how small it is, even though you feel uncomfortable in doing it, it will eventually become something bigger, and they will keep coming back again and again, until you take control of the situation, and put a stop to it, like my wife and I did. When the narcissist leader find a weakness in your life, such as problems or being needy in any area, they will exploit that to control you. If you need finances, they will give you finances and hold it over your head later to control you. If you are having marriage problems, they will bring it up later to you, and will hold it over your head to control you. If you have sinned in anyway, they will bring it up later to you, and will hold it over your head to control you. If they can't control you, they will find a way to get rid of you if you are **lucky**, and I say that because, they really don't want to get rid of you, they really want to keep you under their control for their own self-gain. Remember what Jesus said in **Luke 22 :31** *"And the Lord said, Simon, Simon, behold, Satan hath desired to have you, that he may sift you as wheat."* The narcissist has a desire to have you, and to sift you like wheat. Meaning, to get all that they can get out of you financially, for their own selfish gained. The more people they have under their control, the more finances that will come in, and that means the more finances they can embezzle from the ministry, or organization. Readers, what are we reading about in this book? We are reading about The Modern-Day Pharisees: The Uncovering, how they do their deals in secret, out of the public eyes, how it's all about themselves, and their self-gain, and no one else. I'm talking about a narcissistic leader how they operate. They will say, if you leave this church, and go join another church, you will never see the manifestation of God's blessings come to pass in your life, because your blessings are over here at this church. God said he was going to bless you here, at this church, and not at another. They will make you feel and think that God is only at their church. They will tell you NOT to go and support what other pastors are doing in ministry, because they only want you to hear them and what they have to say so they can control you. You can't let them control you, you have to get control of the situation that you are in so no one will ever be able to exploit it for self-gain. The narcissist leader will always try and make you feel guilty. Don't give them the ammunition to make you feel that way. Own your wrongness, and confess your sins or faults openly, one to another, so that the narcissistic leader can't hold it over you later to control you. If others already know, then there is nothing the narcissist can control you with. The narcissistic leader cannot control the person that is strong spirit, and is confident in themselves, and has high self-esteem. They will try to bully that person to try and break them down to control them. The narcissistic leader will feel very uncomfortable around that person and we'll devise a plan to get rid of them, like my pastors did my wife and me. The narcissistic leader, is very cunning, and self-controlling, and unfortunately, most of the time you don't see it coming until it's there. The more power the narcissist have over you, the more difficult it is for you to break free, and get from under them. A narcissistic leader can be defined as a wolf, in sheep clothing, because they don't feed the flock, they feed on the flock. A narcissistic leader has a destructive pattern of behavior. These leaders crave admiration, and like I said before, they lack empathy for others. Their actions often harm individuals and organizations in many places, even in religious settings. These leaders are often charming. At first they draw people in with big promises, but beneath the surface lies a hunger for control. They use manipulation to get what they want. **True leadership is about service, it's about empowering others**. Narcissistic leadership is the opposite. It's about self-serving motives and exploiting others for your own selfish gain, and we need to understand this type of leadership. We need to learn how to spot it and protect ourselves against it. The narcissistic leader will use manipulation, and control tactics to maintain control over you. They will use many different types of tactics against you. One of the most common tactic is referred to as **gaslighting**. Meaning, to make you question your own sanity, or powers of reasoning. They will sow or plant seeds of doubt in your mind, to make you second-guess yourself, and you say to yourself, did I really say that, or did you really hear me say that? Was I right or was I wrong? Did I really do that? They twist reality and make you question your sanity. <u>They will deny saying things even when you know they did</u>. Another tactic they use is call **triangulation**. This involves bringing a third-party into the conflict. It's a way to control the narrative and make you seem unreasonable to others. They will often use charm and flattery to disarm you. They will use praise one minute, and then turn around and use criticism the next, so you can doubt yourself. **Self-doubt**, and **intimidation**, is another tactic they will use, these are the tools that they use in their arsenal. They might threaten you or spread rumors, or make false accusations against you, to make you look bad, to keep you in line. Remember, these tactics are designed to manipulate you. **Psychological impact** on individuals is another tactic. The impact of narcissistic leadership can be devastating, and victims often experience, anxiety, depression, and low self-esteem. They may doubt their own perceptions and feel constantly on edge. **These leaders create a toxic environment**, where you feel unsafe to speak up, they isolate you from others making you dependent on them only. This can lead to feelings of loneliness and isolation. The constant manipulation can take a toll on your mental and emotional well-being. It's crucial to recognize the signs and take steps to protect yourself. Silence suffering is what they want you to do, and that's why they isolate you from others, but that is not good for you. Narcissism will infiltrate any organization even religious ones. These leaders often use their position of power to exploit others. They might preach about humility while living extravagantly. They may demand, and question your loyalty and obedience, and they might use guilt and shame to control you, or their congregation. This creates an environment of fear and silence. People in this situation often feel trapped. They might fear speaking out against the religious leader because of retribution. Remember, your well-being is important even in a religious context.

Recognizing narcissistic leaders, is the **first step** to protecting yourself. **Pay attention to THEIR ACTIONS, and NOT just their WORDS, because they can be smooth talkers, and suck you right in**. Do they take responsibility for their mistakes, or do they blame others, or do they deflect? You should look for a pattern of grandiosity, and a need for admiration, are they always seeking attention and praise. Do they lack empathy for others? You should notice how they react to criticism, do they become defensive or angry? **If so, these are red flags that should not be ignored**. Let me give you some strategies for dealing with narcissists. Dealing with a narcissistic leader can be challenging, but it's important to set boundaries. Don't engage in their games, or try to reason with them. Stay calm and assertive when communicating with them, and document their behavior, and keep records of interactions, like I did. Don't isolate yourself, but stay connected with supportive friends and family. Remember, you are not alone and help is available. Seeking support and validation is always best, if you are in a bad situation with a narcissistic leader, it's essential to get help, and support. Talk to a therapist or counselor who understands narcissistic abuse. Join a support group and connect with others who have had similar experiences. Remember, it's not your fault. You deserve to be treated with respect and dignity. **Seeking support is a sign of strength, not weakness**. Healing, rebuilding, and moving forward after the storm is essential. Healing from the impact of narcissistic abuse takes time, be patient with yourself and allow yourself to grieve the losses, and the hurt you've experienced. Focus on rebuilding your self esteem, and self worth. Engage in activities that bring you joy, and connect you with others. Remember, you are worthy of love and happiness, you are capable of creating a fulfilling life beyond the influence of a narcissist. Finding your voice again after dealing with a narcissistic leader is very important, and can be very empowering. It can teach you valuable lessons about boundaries, self-respect, and resilience. Use this experience to find your voice and advocate for yourself, and don't be afraid to speak up. Share your story to help others who might be going through something similar. Remember you are stronger than you think, you have the power to break free from toxic relationships, and create a positive future for yourself. Remember the Lord Jesus Christ is your highest authority. **Matthew 28:18** says, *"And Jesus came and spake onto them, saying, all power is given onto me in heaven and in earth."* In Jesus, you have the power, *(authority)* to do all things, and to break free. Be strong and confident in yourself and don't let the narcissist control you. Stand up for yourself, and be the Christian that God called you to be. The warning signs are always there of a narcissistic leader, look for these signs so you can identify them, and stay clear of them.

Chapter 8: Our Covenant

This covenant started in 1997 under my former pastors, and it grew to having fourteen pastors in the covenant, that means fourteen churches was under my former pastors. In 2002, my former pastors formed the Covenant Covering Ministries (CCM) Agreement. My former pastor and his wife, came to North Carolina in March 2002, and set down and talk to my wife and I. They said if we wanted to be under them as a covering, we all had to sign this agreement, but it was a one-sided covenant. The covenant stated that we must support what they are doing physically, and financially, **but it was their choice to support physically or financially what we are doing**. That's not a good covenant. A covenant is an agreement between two or more parties, to support each other, physically and financially, if it came to it, and it's reciprocal. When you are part of a covenant you are supposed to be a team, one together. In a covenant or being a team, you cover me, and I cover you even physically or financially, if it came down to it, that's a team. A team works together in harmony and when there's dis-harmony in a team, it will fall apart, just as our covenant did. Overtime each one left one by one for some reason or another, but let my pastors tell it, it was always something that that pastor and his wife was doing, or wasn't doing. My former pastor and his wife would always blame the leaving on the person that left. Those of us that remain in the covenant, my former pastors would always come back and talk about the pastor and his wife that left. They would talk to us that was still in the covenant, and would put those people down, in such ways, as though they were not Christians, and called them everything but a child of God. They would always tell us, don't call those people that left, don't contact them for any reason, don't even talk to them if they call you. I often wondered why, but it wasn't until we were dismissed from the covenant ourselves, and I was able to go back and talk to some of those pastors, and people that left the covenant. That's when I found out that the things that my former pastor said about those people was not true. They said, what had actually happen was, my former pastors had created a very toxic environment, the way they talk to and treated people, and that's not good, and we told them we no longer wanted to be a part of that. It's always two sides to every story. Things were fabricated by my former pastors to make the other pastor and his wife look bad, and to make it look like that my former pastor and his wife was right. I have to say, and I agree the environment had become very toxic. Eventually it got down to just two pastors under my former pastors, my wife and I, and the other pastors that is from a church south of Atlanta. Now I'm no genius but out of twelve pastors leaving, you can't tell me that it was always the person fault that left. The only common denominator in all fourteen of us, is my former pastor and his wife, but like I stated earlier, they can't do no wrong, let them tell it, they have never done any wrong, every time someone left it wasn't their fault, so they say. Every pastor that have left this covenant for what ever reason, my former pastor's wife has gossiped about them. She has always called my wife and I, probably the other pastors also, when someone leave, and told us her reason why that person or persons left. She would tell us those people personal business, what was or had been going on in their marriages. Pastors and future leaders, why tell someone else's business, it has no redemptive value, it's already done and over, and by telling someone else, is not going to change the fact that it has already happen. As their spiritual leader, you should pray for them and not talk about them. So I would say to her, why tell us? She would use the statement: "I just think you all should know." WHY? That's their business, and no one else, and I would say to myself, it's just her way of gossiping. Pastors why tell someone's personal business, they trusted you in the first place by telling you, and again, it has no redemptive value telling others, and by telling someone else's business, it's not going to change things. Pastors it's just your way to gossip, and you trying to make yourself feel good by saying, I just thought you should know, that's a cop out, and a lame excuse, stop gossiping. My wife and I told her, stop telling us other people's business, we don't care to know, that's between them, and God. The only way you can stop gossipers, is to cut them off. It doesn't matter who you are or what your title is or what position you hold, as long as they have someone that will listen to them they will gossip. What are we reading about in this book? The Modern-Day Pharisees, The Uncovering, and it shows, no matter who you are, or what's your title is you are subject to do wrong, and try an justify it. We all were in this covenant together as a team, and a team always have a leader, and the leader must take responsibility for the team's action, and not put it off on someone else. Let me say this, as a former military leader, and a pastor, I have learned that the road to opportunity through others, is often the road that is most overlooked by leaders, because they think God can only use them, and they miss the help that God has set before them, to help them carry out, or accomplished the mission, or vision. Success of failure of a team always points back to the leader's leadership ability of the team. Every team has a leader, and that leader job is to keep the team together by teaching the team how to work together, as a team. There are no individuals when it comes to a team. If the team failed, it failed as a team, and not as an individual. In order for a team to be successful, it has to know its purpose, the bible call it vision. **Proverbs 29:18** says, *"Where there is no vision, the people perish... ."* The leader of the team failed us when it came to vision, and that's why the team over the years fell apart. After the Covenant Covering Ministries (CCM) Agreement was signed, you never heard anything else about the vision for CCM. The Holy Spirit instructed, my wife and I not to leave, stay put, and once again God revealed, the true hearts of my former pastors. I wish you readers could hear the recording that I made of my former pastor and his wife, after they dismissed us. They let us have it! My former pastor's wife was mad! I don't know why she was so mad, I guess because I told her in time past, that she **"bully"** people, so I guess she figured she'll just let me have it before I left. She said, "yes I was mad! **I was beyond mad**, calling me out of my name, calling me a bully. That's not my name!". So in the process of dismissing us, she felt as though she will just let me have it. She called herself really telling me off for calling her out of her name. She really is acting like a bully, just listen to how she is talking and acting, which is the action of a bully when you stand up to them. So whether I called her a bully or not, what's the difference? When a person is this mad, they will say and do anything to get back at someone. But didn't God say in **1 Thessalonians 5:15,** *"See that none render evil for evil unto any man; but ever follow that which is good, both among yourselves, and to all men."* This was just a plain case of abuse of power, that goes on in the churches today. And that's what this book is all about, The Modern-Day Pharisees: The Uncovering, how they abuse their power, position, and title, and how they treat the people any way they see fit, because they have the power to do so, and they think they can get away with it. But listen to what God said in **Micah 2:1,** *"Woe to them that devise iniquity, and work evil upon their beds! when the morning is light, they practice it,* **because it is in the power of their hand."** In other words, God says you do it because you think you can get away with it, because it is in your power to do it. But he says, woe! meaning it's a warning, there is going to be a day of punishment for your actions. As a leader, people deserve to be treated with dignity and respect. So, they dismissed us, we did not leave on our own. **I can only imagine what they have said about my wife and I, the reason why we left, just like she did talking**

to us about the other pastors that left. But who cares! I know she told some fabricated, untrue story, because that's who she is, <u>but remember they dismissed us, we didn't leave on our own</u>. She felt as though, she really told us off. She told us, we thought we was better than they are. You all may have money, and you all may have a new church building, but you know what, we have the presence of God. I said to myself wow, are you implying that we don't have the presence of God at our church? Are you implying that God would build a brand-new building, God did it not us, and not put His presence there. I said to myself, you are some piece of work. This is what I'm talking about, this is the type of verbal abuse that we have endured for the last two years, and you wonder why people leave a ministry with leadership like this. I said every time someone leave the ministry, or you ask someone to leave, is never you all's fault, it's always someone else's fault. I said you all have turned into someone, that I can't even recognize anymore. I know she was recording, because she kept trying to draw me into an argument, but I just wouldn't fall for it. If she had drawn me into an argument, she would've played the recording for the other pastors later and says see, that's what I'm talking about, listen to him, no respect, and no honor. She was recording without our permission, and doing it illegally, because she was in a country that first requires permission to record someone's conversation. But that's the type of person she is, the rules or laws don't apply to her. This is the same thing she did while in the military, she just think rules and regulations don't pertain to her, so she just do what she want, and that's why when she was in the military, she was punished and demoted to a lower rank.

Now, let me say this about recording someone's conversation. Laws vary from state to state, so make sure you look up the law for your state before recording someone's conversation, as I did. In the state of North Carolina, where I live, you don't have to inform the person that you are recording them. North Carolina is considered a **one party**, or a **single party** state, meaning you **DON'T** have to inform the person or persons, that you are recording. If you have informed someone, that I'm going to record this conversation, they now have a responsibility to themselves at that time to stop talking if they don't want what they said recorded. If they keep talking, that's on them, because you have informed them of your intentions. It's the same as when a police officer read you your rights, *"you have the right to remain silent, anything you say can, and will be held against you in a court of law... ."* You have the right at that point to stop talking, and not say anything else, but if you keep talking, because of your arrogance, whatever you say, will be held against you in a court of law, and that's on you, because you can't control your mouth to stop talking. The problem I see with most people when you inform them that you're going to record them, they are so arrogant, or mad, they will say *I don't care what you do,* because they think you're really not going to record them. With technology today, all it takes is an app on your phone, and press it to start recording, but arrogant, mad, and prideful people don't think you will. I want you to know, I have no intent of releasing these recordings at this time, that is not my purpose in recording, or writing this book. **These recordings is only evidence, and <u>proof for myself</u> about what has been going on for years in ministry**.

As pastors, we have great authority over the lives of others, and that authority, comes with great responsibility to do the right thing at all times, at all costs, and in every situation no matter what. Pastors, you should lead by precept and examples, that others may follow, and not just go along to get along. When we get it wrong, or do the wrong thing, we should be quick to confess it, and ask God for forgiveness, so that He can continue to bless our ministry. It's important that you let your people know that you were wrong when you thought you was right. It let them know that you're human, and your subject to mistakes. In everything we should be a good example before the flock at all times, and in everything, that others would follow. Like I said before, my former pastors turn into someone that I can't recognize anymore.

Let me give you a BIG word that describes my former pastors **action**. Do you know what the word **Prevarication** means? Quick definition. It means *"the act of lying, a false or deliberate misstatement."* That's what my former pastors had turned into, liars, making false or deliberate, misstatements trying to make us look bad because I said, his wife act like a bully. Let me tell you about the biggest fabrication that my former pastor's wife told about me, and she did it openly on zoom with the other pastors on also, and said it was from God. Listen to this, this is what she said to me in an email, after she talked about it on zoom. This is a copy of the actual email that she sent to me, typos and all.

Let me say this before we read this email. Be careful who you allow to speak into your life. You have to know that that person is a true prophet or prophetess from God and has your best interest at heart. And not someone that is holding something against you, and just trying to find a way to get back at you. A true prophet or prophetess will know things about you supernaturally, they will be able to walk up to you and read you like a book without asking you questions about yourself. I've had someone on different occasions, in different churches, to do that to me, and they did not ask me a bunch of questions first. Remember in chapter two, I told you about the Court-Martial trial I went through when I was in the military? I went to church one Sunday morning while going through this Court-Martial, and a prophetess called me out, and said to me, *"what you are going through, the Lord said, stand your ground, stand still, God has already fought the battle for you, and have given you the victory."* She didn't know anything about me, or what I was going through. She didn't know me from Adam. She didn't ask me a bunch of questions first, to find out what I was going through. She just looked at me and spoke out what the Holy Spirit gave her, which was exactly true, there was no way for her to know that I was going through a Court-Martial. Remember, I stood my ground, and I was found not guilty in that Court-Martial trial. Now that was a true prophecy. The Lord was giving me words of encouragement through that prophetess, that I have the victory. Like I said earlier, a true prophet, or prophetess, will know things about you supernaturally, that only the Holy Spirit could reveal, and as she spoke it, I knew it was true. They won't have to use gimmicks, games and tricks the prophesy to you. I've seen so-called prophets and prophetess, call people out in the congregation, and they start out by asking them questions. They say there is something you've been going through, is something you've been dealing with, and when they finally hit the right question, and you comment on it, they say, that's it. That's what it is, and I know the Lord has been dealing with you about that. They say, that's what the Lord showed me about you, and the Lord said you need to do dus-in-so. They play on people emotions, and that's not prophesying. You just asking someone a few questions to find out some things about them. A true Prophet or prophetess would know things about you supernaturally. If you have 500 people sitting in the sanctuary, and you said the Lord spoke to me and said someone in here is having back pains, or someone in here is having problems with your knees, or someone in here is having migraine headaches. Really! Are you for real! You know you will have at least fifty people out of 500 setting in the sanctuary with one of these three problems. Back or knee pains, and or headaches are very common, and you use this to convince people that you are a prophet, or prophetess prophesying. A true prophet, or prophetess will know things about you supernaturally, there is no way that person could have known that about you, except it comes from God, and they won't have to ask you a bunch of questions before they start prophesying over you.

Ok, back to the email. My former pastor's wife said the Lord spoke to her and this is what the Lord showed her about me. I don't believe the Lord showed her any such thing. Remember, she said earlier in this chapter, "yes, I was mad, **I was beyond mad!** Calling me out of my name, calling me a bully." I believe this email is just her way of getting back at me for calling her out of her name, as she said. So, as you read or listen to this email, I want you to listen to how envy, and jealous she has become because of me and my wife's accomplishments. My wife and I are totally debt free, earlier this year 2025, we paid off our home mortgage years early, and we owe no one anything. Over the years through the teaching of the word of God based on faith, my wife and I have learned to live above debt, and the cares of this world. We have been in debt, and it does not feel good, but now we are debt free, and all my former pastor's wife can find, is faults, by saying that we brag about what we have. The ministry that God has placed me over as pastor, is debt free, I draw no salary from my church, the new building is paid for in full, the ministry owes no one anything. When my wife and I, talk about the goodness of God in our lives, and what he has done for us, we are not bragging, we are only giving a good report of what the Lord has done for us, and it is only done to encourage others, that the Lord will do it for them also. But I see those that are envy and jealous of others will always call it bragging, and put them down. She does that simply because I told her she bully people, and that's not right to do that. So she writes an email to me, and said it's from the Lord, to put down my church, my new church building, my automobiles, my home, my position as a pastor, my education, my finances, and all that God has blessed me and my wife with. I believe that this is envy, and jealousy at it's highest level. So I encourage you as you read or listen to this email, listen to the fruits that has been produced here, you be the judge. Jesus said in **Matthew 7:16** *"you shall know them by their fruits."* I believe this is what is in her heart, to try and discredit me, because of my accomplishments, and **because I am outspoken when it comes to wrongness, no matter who it is**. Look what Jesus says here in **Matthew 15:19-20** *"For out of the heart proceed <u>evil thoughts</u>... these are the things which defile a man... ."* It is demonic when you allow yourself to sit and think about how you are going to get back at others and try and discredit them. **James 1:19-20** says, *"Wherefore, my beloved brethren, let every man be swift to hear, slow to speak, slow to wrath: for the wrath of man worketh not the righteousness of God."* Jesus said, that the wrath of man is not of God, it is a condition of the heart, and He said it is evil when you do something like this. **Listen to this email she wrote, and how <u>envy, and jealous</u> it sounds of my accomplishments, so she has to make it**

sound spiritual in order to put me down. She has to make it sound like it came from God, when in fact, it actually came from the movies, and I will show you this later.

"Jake
Spiritual Connotation: New Covenant
Scripture: Colossians 3:11 The Living Bible (TLB)
In this new life one's nationality or race or education or social position is unimportant. Whether a person has Christ is what matters.

Jake was in his office, and the church preparing for Sunday when he heard a noise in the sanctuary. He arose from his desk, to investigate what was happening. He called out" Who is there" He looked around and did not see anyone. Suddenly a bright light filled the sanctuary. It was so bright it blinded Jake for a moment. Jesus walked out of the light. Hello Jake, I thought we would have a little talk Jake just stood there not believing that this was happening. He rubbed his eyes making sure he was not seeing things. It is me Jake said Jesus. Jesus began to walk toward Jake "I would like to ask you a question. If I asked you to give up all of this, your new church building, your educational achievements, your financial standing, your status as a pastor. Would you do it for me? "Of course," said Jake. "Jesus you are my everything," Really? said Jesus and before Jake could answer he was in another place. He recognized it was his church, but somehow it different. He did not know anyone there. The sanctuary was filled with people, and everyone was full of joy praising the Lord. Someone walked up to Jake and said Hi Welcome to Jesus

World Outreach Center, my name is William and what is your name? My name is Dr. Jake Williams pastor of this church. I have never seen you before, and why are you ushering? I did not authorize this. "Well Jake....we do not want any problems here, I just wanted to welcome you on the behalf of our pastor. Pastor Lemuel is that man on the stage." Another man walked up and said, "Is everything okay Willliam" "This is Jake" My name is Dr. Jake Williams; this is my building. Do you know what I went through to have this building? You do not understand who you talking to. The man called a couple other people over and escorted Jake outside of the building. "If you come back in, we will call the police," said the man Dejected Jake went looking for his car. "Where is my car?" He pulled his key and click the unlock button. He heard the click behind him. Turning around he saw the ugliest grey car he had ever seen. "This cannot be my car" He walked around the car, it had dinks and pings in various places of the car. To top it off it was dirty. Jake pulled the door open and loud screeched sounded. "No, no, no," said Jake. He got into his car and drove home. "Please let me have the same house, please! He pulled up in front of his house. As he was walking up to his house the door opened and their stood his wife. "Hey Jake, how was your day?" Terrible, I went to the church to get some work done and another pastor was on the stage getting ready to preach. This Pastor Lemuel, whatever his name is has our church. "What are you talking about?" said his wife "We don't have a church and we are not pastors" "Not you too!" shouted Jake. "We do have a church; you are a pastor, and I am a pastor.

We both have our degrees. "Speaking of degrees," said his wife. "You had another rejection letter from the school. "Rejection letter, I have already been to school and graduated." "I know you are speaking by faith Jake, and besides, we really do not have enough money in the bank "No this is not by faith I have it now and what do you mean we do not have enough money in the bank. Where is my money, where is my car, where is my church, what is going on? Jake fell to his knees with his face in his hands. "I thought that these things did not matter to you Jake?" said Jesus Jake looked up and saw he was back in the sanctuary with Jesus. "I did not know you were going to take it all away from me. "I did not take it from you. You gave it to me, I asked you would you give up the building, educational success and your status and you said yes. When you give something to me, it belongs to me, it is no longer yours. This showed what is in your heart. What is more important me or those things? Jesus hit Jake in the chest and his spirit flew out of his body. Jake was in midair. Tell me said Jesus what can you accomplish without me? Then Jesus pulled him back into his body. Do not brag of your wisdom or the great things that have been done through you. Do not brag about how much money you have and tag a spiritual comment, the Lord blessed me. If you want to brag about anything brag of this and this only: That you understand and know me. I'm GOD, and I act in loyal love. I do what is right and set things right and fair, and delight in those who do the same things. These are my trademarks." Who are you without those things Jake. Those things do not make you, said Jesus. I make you by my Spirit.

There are no substitutes. When you let go of yourself then you can truly embrace me with all of your heart. When do that, look at all the great things we can do together. All sudden Jake was back sitting at his desk where he started."

    <u>Doesn't this really sound ridiculous?</u> And doesn't this email sounds like a person that is really envy, and jealous of others accomplishments? Shame on you Pastor! **Ephesians 4:31-32** says, "*Let all bitterness, and wrath, and anger, and clamour, and evil speaking, <u>be put away from you</u>, with all malice: and be ye kind one to another, tenderhearted, forgiving one another, even as God for Christ's sake hath forgiven you.*" And **Hebrews 13:5** says, "*...be content with such things **as ye have**...* ." You don't know what that person had to go through to get to, or to have the things that they have? So why put them down and try and make it sound like God is speaking. No, this was not from God, this was all flesh! **Now, by my former pastor's wife, own admission, they are satisfied with minimum education and did not seek anything higher. Just because you refused higher education, and did not want anything better, you should not condemn those that desired, and sought more to be better in life**. Anyone reading this email can see that the Holy Spirit has not showed her anything of the sort, **<u>this was all flesh</u>**. Didn't Jesus say in **Matthew 24:4-11** "*...Take heed that no man deceive you. And many false prophets shall rise,* *and shall deceive many."* And in **Matthew 7:15-16** Jesus said, *"Beware of false prophets, which come to you in sheep's clothing, but inwardly they are ravening wolves. <u>Ye shall know them by their fruits</u>... ."* These type of people that self promote themselves and give themselves a title, calling themselves prophet or prophetess, can only produce corrupt fruit. They were never called to that position by God, because you can tell by the fruits that they produce. Jesus said *"you shall know them by their fruits."* The fruit of their labor is the fruits of **deception, jealousy, envy, division** and **discord**, and if you stand back and observe them, you can see it. **If you go back and read this email again and pay very close attention, you can plainly see these fruits in this email.** Jesus went on to say in **Matthew 7: 21-23,** *"Not every one that saith unto me, Lord, Lord, shall enter into the kingdom of heaven; but he that doeth the will of my Father which is in heaven. Many will say to me in that day, Lord, Lord, have we not prophesied in thy name? and in thy name have cast out devils? and in thy name done many wonderful works? And then will I profess unto them, **I never knew you:** depart from me, ye that work iniquity."* The reason why Jesus said *"<u>I never knew you</u>,"* is because God is a God of love, and Jesus is saying to the false prophet or prophetess, you didn't walk in love, or show love by your actions, so *"depart from me, ye that work iniquity."* **Iniquity means, unfair behavior, wickedness, or sin**. It is not love when all you can do is find fault in others, what they have, and what they do. A

false prophet or prophetess is an opportunitess, they wait and look for an opportunity to deceive others. This email is no prophecy, or spiritual connotation from God. This is a person that has their heart set on making me look like someone that brags about my accomplishments. This is someone that really, really, really, really, really wants to put down someone's else accomplishments. Readers I want you to know, I have never bragged about any of my accomplishments. I have done some extraordinary things in my military career and life that some people can only dream of doing. But one thing I have never done, is bragged, because I know where my blessings come from. I give God all the praise, and thanks, for being able to accomplish these things, because they was not done of myself, but God working through me. Now, how is it that she as my leader, that is supposed to be my spiritual guide, can be so spiritual, and a prophetess, but yet has such a hard heart towards me, because I said you bully people. I don't know how a person can be so spiritual, but can not see all the blessings of God that is going on around me and my wife life, and our ministry, but all you can find is fault. That is beyond my comprehensions, when you can see the hand of God on others, but refuse to acknowledge it or accept it, but instead put it down. But this is the same thing that Paul and Barnabas went through in the book of Acts when they taught in the synagogue. **Acts 13:44-45** says, *"And the next sabbath day came **almost the whole city** together to hear the word of God. But when the Jews saw the multitudes, they were* *filled with **envy**, and spake against those things which were spoken by Paul, contradicting and blaspheming."* Pastors and future leaders, we are no different than Paul and Barnabas. When you do good things, or have things, people will envy you and speak against you, so pay them no attention. Case in point; listen to this. It says in **Genesis 26:12-14** *"Then Isaac sowed in that land, and received in the same year an hundredfold: and **the LORD blessed him**. And the man waxed great, and went forward, and grew until he **became very great:** for he had possession of flocks, and possession of herds, and great store of servants: and the **Philistines envied him**."* When the Lord bless you, like He did Isaac, and you have something in life, **they're going to be those that will envy you**, because of what you have. There will always be haters, and critics, and it will come from the person that you would have never expected it to come from, but remember, Jesus said in **Matthews 12:34** *"...out of the abundance of the heart the mouth speaketh."* That means envy, and jealousy was in that person's heart the whole time, and you can't hide what's in your heart. I encourage you to hold your peace when people speak against you. Don't be so quick to open your mouth and try to defend yourself when people lie on you, let the Lord fight the battle for you. He can't fight the battle for you if you are too busy trying to fight it yourself, so in return God takes his hands off of it, and let you fight it. **1 Peter 5:6-7** says, *"Humble yourselves therefore under the mighty hand of God, that he may exalt you in due time. Casting all your care* *upon him; for he careth for you."* **Psalms 34:19** says, *"Many are the afflictions of the righteous: but the LORD delivereth him out of them all."* Notice what the Lord said. He did not say He is going to deliver you, He said, He has **already** delivered you **from them all**. Sometime it might take a while for truth to come out, or victory to come, but the Lord **HAS** delivered us from all things that will come against you. God is always on the side of what is truth and what is right, and truth always has a way of coming to the light when you cast **your care** on the Lord. This email is from a person that is full of themselves, and full of envy, and pride, and truly need prayer, so that their eyes are open, so that they will see where they have errored. You can tell that this email comes from someone this is bitter, and jealous, who only has, by her own admission, her and her husband a high school education, and is envy of my wife and I accomplishments. Now, don't get me wrong! I know people personally, and all they have is a high school education, and they are very successful in life, because they are guided, and directed by the Holy Spirit, in all they do. But I also know that that is not true in all cases, because of the condition of the person's heart. If a high school education is all you want that's fine, but don't put my wife, me, and others down because we desired more. Pastors, knowledge is power, and I'm referring to **spiritually**, and **secular**. As leaders, you should always be striving to learn more to be better in all that you do, so you don't have to depend on others. Don't just be satisfied where you are, because God has given you so much more. When you have knowledge, you have power, and no one can ever take it from you. Pastors, I believe you should educate yourself beyond a high school education, because there are going to be people that come into your ministry that is educated, and some will be highly educated, and you will always find fault in those people because you're not. You might not ever say it, but you will always feel jealous, and intimidated around those people, so in return you will bully them because of your position and title. But just as I said earlier in this chapter, **Micah 2:1** says, *"...you do it, because it's in the power of your hand."* But there's going to be a day of punishment for your actions. There will always be those that will put down your education, but pay them no attention. Knowing when to remain silent when others are speaking against you is power, because remaining silent is the best reply to foolish talking. Some people will say or do whatever it takes to get you to act out of character, but don't give them the satisfaction of provoking you to do that. The less you respond to negative people, the more peaceful your life will become. As a pastor, I have learned over these thirty six years in ministry, and twenty eight years of pastoring, that being silent and observing, often reveals more about a person than a thousand words spoken by them. Being silent isn't weakness, is strategy. Sometime God will show you what you need to see and not what to say. Don't let your need to be heard, miss your moment to be effective. Sometime you can't be effective with others, is because you always have too much to say. Remember I brought out earlier in this chapter in **James 1:19** it says, *"...let every man be swift to hear, and slow to speak... ."* I encourage you to know when to remain silent and calm, but also know when to speak up. When you learn to do that, you have learned to operate with wisdom. Wisdom is the application of knowledge, and knowledge is power, and that's why it's important that you educate yourself. But on the other hand, ignorance is the absence of knowledge, and it will hinder or destroy you, and keep you in bondage, because you can't operate in something that you have no knowledge in. **Hosea 4:6** says, *"My people are destroyed for lack of knowledge: because thou hast rejected knowledge, I will also reject thee, that thou shalt be no priest to me: seeing thou hast forgotten the law of thy God, I will also forget thy children."* God said, people are destroyed for one reason, and one reason <u>ONLY</u>, **a lack of knowledge**, and that's in anything. Now, can you see the importance of education? My former pastors have never pushed themselves to be better, and this email is from someone who I believe is bitter, and could not have her way with me, because I am confident, and strong spirited. She has always spoke down about me and my wife accomplishments, but that's all right because we know who we are in Christ. This is the modern-day Pharisee, how they publicly put others down, to make themselves look good, and appear righteous to others. Since March 2020, she has always spoke down about our new church building, because my former pastor, her husband was not the guest speaker, <u>so she thought</u>, **but if they had just shown up to support us, he would have been the guest speaker.** So, in one of our Monday morning teachings on zoom, she told us the story that you just read or heard in this email and then later she emailed it to me. It is a sad state, and a sad place to be, when you can't be happy for other people's accomplishment, but instead you fabricate stories to put them down to try and make them look bad and say it's from the Lord. That is a sad place especially when you are a minister of the gospel, and a prophetess. But the bible warns us about false ministers, and false prophets and prophetess, it is not just for old times, they are still alive today, and are very active. This book is about The Modern-Day Pharisees: The Uncovering, how these things still go on today, but hidden, and undercover, and you need to be aware of it. The bible says in **Revelation 2:20** *"...that woman Jezebel, which calleth herself a prophetess... ."* Noticed God didn't say He called her a prophetess; He said that woman Jezebel, called **herself, herself, herself**, I want you to get it, **she called herself a prophetess**. That means she was self promoted, like a lot of spiritual leaders do today. You have to be mindful of who is trying to speak into your life, and you have to be mindful to try the spirit by the Spirit, and not let the wrong spirit try to speak something into your life. False prophets and prophetess always have a word for others, but they can't receive a word from anyone because they think they only hear from God, and that's foolishness! That's not discernment that's pride at its highest level. True prophets don't just hear from God, they hear God in others. False prophets are not accountable to anyone, and they will not be submitted. They don't receive correction, and they don't seek counsel from others, but they want everybody else to submit to them and their prophetic word, that's not prophecy that's narcissistic. Everyone has to submit to someone. Even Jesus himself as a boy, submitted and sit under the teachers in the synagogue, even though they couldn't teach him anything because He is all knowing, and He was God in the flesh. But I believe this was an illustration of being submitted under authority to the leaders in the synagogue. Throughout the bible, there are illustrations of people that are in leadership position being under the authority of someone. Moses had Jethro, Samuel answer to Eli, Elisha submitted to and served Elijah, Paul submitted to the council and teaching of Priscilla and Aquila. Paul also submitted to Ananias and the Apostles, Timothy submitted to Paul, and Joseph submitted to Pharaoh. Everyone had someone to submit to, but here you are, apart of the five-fold ministry, but unsubmitted and answers to no one, but yet call yourself a prophet or prophetess. Every Spirit-led person need structure, they need someone to answer to, they need a role model, and they need training. The truth is, you hide behind the phrase, **"God told me this about you,"** when you are talking to others, so no one will challenge you. You use prophecy as a shield to defend your actions, so that you don't have to walk in love or relationship with others. A true prophet walk in humility and knows how to submit, and they know how to receive as much as they release to others, but a false prophet or prophetess and narcissistic leaders doesn't. They sow discord, and use isolation to separate others, so the truth about your deeds, won't come out. Bishop Demetrius J. Sinegal said, "If you're to anointed to be accountable, to gifted to be guided, to selfish to be submitted, and to prophetic to be shepherd, you're not a prophet or prophetess, **you're a problem**." What he just said is absolutely the truth, and I agree 100%. If you can't submit yourself, and sit under someone, **you are a problem**. A person with this type of spirit need to sit down and let God deal with that Jezebel spirit which is upon you, and the parts of you that think that you are always supposed to be out front in the spotlight. You can't be a prophet or prophetess or apart of the five-fold ministry and be unteachable. If you are not under authority, or have never sit under authority, and was not sent by God, but just went on your own, you are not qualified to be in the position of authority. If you are a leader over the lives of others, you must be under authority, if not you will abuse your people and all that you have. So I will say this to you the reader, or listener, if you as a pastor have never sit under authority, to be submitted to it, there's no way that you know what it means to submit to the authority that is over you. Everyone needs somebody, so submit yourself to someone.

    Now, going back to the email. No, I don't receive what she had to say physically, spiritually or in this email because I know who I am in Christ, and whom I am, I'm His. I believe I am doing what God has called me to do, and that's why He has blessed my wife and I along the way. This is what she emailed me, saying the spirit of the Lord spoke to her. **This is <u>NOT</u> from the Spirit of the Lord, it's FROM THE MOVIES.** Remember, I told you earlier I will show you where she got this from, well here it is, **<u>it's from this movie</u>**. If you go back and read this and look at this email, when she said, *"Jesus hit Jake in the chest and his spirit flew out of his body. Jake was in midair."* It doesn't take a PhD degree to know where she got this from, if you have never seen this movie, go look at this movie called **"<u>Avengers: Endgame</u>,"** that's where that came from. ***"It was the scene where they were looking for the time stone, and the Hulk approach the female monk that had the time stone around her neck. When he tried to get the time stone, she hit the Hulk in his chest and knocked his spirit out of his body. She actually knocked Bruce Banner out of the Hulk's body, and he floated there in the air before coming down, and when he came down, they walked around talking."*** <u>That's where she got this from</u>. So, you get your material from the movies, and try to put a spiritual twist on it, to make yourself look spiritual, and call yourself a prophetess, and say it's from God. Wow! Pastors, and church leaders, when you do something like this, saying it's from God, when it is not, but, it's from the movies, and you put it in writing for all to see, you are only discrediting yourself, as a minister of the gospel and a prophetess. The devil doesn't have to discredit you, you have done it to yourself. **If you don't know it, know this, that Christians watch movies also**. We were on zoom one Monday morning and my former pastor's wife told me, *that she is my arch nemesis just like the villain in the movie Spider-Man.* What a shameful thing to say to one of your leaders, we're not against each other we are supposed to be on the same team, so I thought. One thing I've learned in this covenant relationship, people can say whatever they want to say about you, but just because they said it, doesn't make it true, even if they **tag** it with **"the Lord said."** You can become a better you, by distancing yourself from these type of people, or relationships, no matter who they are, or what their title is. You don't need to be around people like this, and do not pour anymore of yourself, or the good that you do into a relationship that lacks the capacity to pour good back into you, because eventually you will be left EMPTY, so just move on.

Let me tell you something about leadership, that you might not know. **You can't lead what you don't like**. If you don't like a person, or people, there's no way you can lead them, I should know, I spent twenty-two years in the military, and twenty of those years were leading people. That is a poor leader to make these types of statements, about people they are supposed to be leading. I wanted to tell her, she needs to stay out of the movies trying to get her material, because it's not working for you, but out of respect, I wouldn't say it. I have learned with my former pastors, sometimes you just have to smile and wave, and just let words like that roll off of your back, like a duck in water. This email is written from someone that I believe that has not gotten over something that has happened to them in their past, and has become twisted in their thinking. Remember I brought out in chapter six, when she was in the military, she was punished, and demoted back down to a lower rank because of her conduct, and that can be devastating to a person. Because of that, she may have low self-esteem, envy, and is jealous of other people's accomplishments, and that is what's causing her to act out in this way, because that is what's in her heart, and you can't hide what's in your heart. The devil will always try an use someone to do his dirty work, but know that the Lord has delivered you from all his tricks. **Psalm 34:19** says, *"Many are the afflictions of the righteous: But the LORD delivereth him out of them all."* When a person allows evil thoughts and ideas to get down into their heart they will carry them out to get back at others, and that is what defiles you. **Matthew 15:19-20** says, *"For out of the heart proceed evil thoughts..., ...these are the things which defile a man."* Jesus said your evil thoughts that you have in your heart against others is what corrupts you. Remember what Jesus said about the heart in **Matthew 12:34-37,** He said, *"O generation of vipers, how can ye, being evil, speak good things? for out of the abundance of the heart the mouth speaketh. A good man out of the good treasure of the heart bringeth forth good things: and an evil man out of the evil treasure bringeth forth evil* *things. But I say unto you, That every idle word that men shall speak, they shall give account thereof in the day of judgment. For by thy words thou shalt be justified, and by thy words thou shalt be condemned."* Notice what Jesus said, an evil person out of the evil treasures of their heart can only bring fourth evil things. Jesus is letting us know, that it all comes down to the condition of your heart, and that you are going to give an account for your actions, and every idle or useless word that you have done to or have spoken to others, you will be judged for it. He is letting us know that the words that we speak is going to **justify us** *(which means to make <u>righteous</u>)* or they're going to **condemn us** *(which means <u>punishment</u>)*. You will always give an account for the words that you speak, because **Isaiah 55:11** says, *"So shall my word be that goeth forth out of my mouth: it shall not return onto me void, but it shall accomplish that which I please, and it shall prosper, in the thing whereto I sent it."* **Proverbs 18:21** says, *"that death and life is in the power of the tongue."* The power is always in what you say, and if you say anything that is opposite of what God has said in His word, is what condemns you. The Amplified Bible in **Jeremiah 1:12** says *"...I am [actively] watching over My word to fulfill it."* God is watching and waiting for you to speak and do His word, so he can fulfill it. **James 2:20** says, *"...that faith without works is dead."* If you don't speak or do what God has said there's nothing for Him to fulfill. God can only perform or fulfill His word. He does not fulfill what you think or feel, only His word.

One day I was in my office, and sitting behind my desk talking to my former pastor and his wife on zoom, and all of my diplomas and certificates on my wall behind me can be clearly seen. She saw them, and from that day forward, for the next two years, she has always downed my wife and I concerning our advanced education, our accomplishments, and all that God has blessed us with, **and you can see this plainly in this email**. She would say things like, it's not about your education, you thank you are something because you all have your doctorate degrees, you need to take that down off the wall because that's just pride. Now readers, let me ask you this question. Who goes to school or college, and complete their degrees and put them in a folder and put them in a desk drawer? No one! Everyone that I know, that has completed their higher education, even their high school education, has taken their diplomas, or degrees and have put them on the wall, because they are proud of their, and their children's accomplishments. That's the only reason why we put them on the wall, <u>proud</u>, **NOT PRIDE!** Again, what am I talking about in this book? I am talking about The Modern-Day Pharisees: The Uncovering, how they will abuse their authority, and try an force there will upon others, to make you do what they want you to do, and hide these actions from others. My wife and I never paraded around and bragged about our degrees. We just thank God that He blessed us to be able to complete them, because, like I stated earlier, when I graduated high school in 1975 at age seventeen, I was not college material. In other words, I just barely got out of high school, and there was no way I was academically ready for college, and it took years for me to be ready. We thank God and praise Him for the new church building, that He blessed us with, pay for in full. We thank God that he blessed us with a mind, and education to be able to invest in stocks and bonds, CDs and other investments, to have money, and not have to draw a salary from the church. Twenty-seven years of pastoring, and I've never had to draw a salary from the church but for only three months, what a blessing! God has blessed my wife and I greatly, and we praise God for that! We've always and will continue to give a good report about what God has done in our lives, and it's not bragging. It's amazing how church leaders that is against you, can call it bragging when you talk about what God has done or bless you with. But on the other hand, when **THEY** talk about what God has done or bless **THEM** with, THEY CALL IT A TESTIMONY. It's all done in favor for themselves, but for others is called bragging so it will make them look bad to others. But that is what we're talking about in this book the modern day Pharisee, how is all about making themselves look good in front of the people, and to make others to look bad. Pastors and church leaders, stop being so judgmental when it comes to others. Isn't that's what praise and testimony is all about in church, so others can hear, and see what God has done for someone? Yes, so it will motivate them to get in church and learn, so God can do it for them also. When my wife and I talk about the goodness of God, and all He's done, it's called, giving a good report, of what God has done, it's not bragging, and it's not pride. Jesus talks about giving a good report in the book of **Mark 5:19-20,** "Jesus had cast out the unclean spirits out of the man, and the man wanted to go with Jesus, but Jesus told him no, but go home until your friends, how great thing the Lord has done for him, and had compassion on him. The bible says that the man departed and begin to publish abroad how great things Jesus had done for him, and had compassion on him, and all men did marvel at what he said." Now that's a good report, that's not bragging. **It's what Jesus told the man, and us to do, go give a good report, of what the Lord has done for you.** So, when my wife and I talk about what the Lord has done for us, we are not bragging, but when you're jealous of other people's accomplishment, and what they have, you will call it bragging, because that's all you can see, because of the condition of your heart. Listen to what God says in **1 Timothy 6:17**, He said, *"Charge them that are rich in this world, that they be not highminded, nor trust in uncertain riches,* **but in the living God, <u>who giveth us richly all things to enjoy</u>**.*"* God said in this scripture, let them that have something in this world know, not to have such high moral principles, that you are no earthly good to anyone but yourself. He said, don't trust in your riches, because they're here today and could be gone tomorrow. He said put your faith and trust in the living God, who gives you richly **all things, all things, all things, all things,** I want you to get what God is saying, who gives you richly **all things, "<u>to enjoy</u>."** That's powerful! God has given us, those that have obeyed His Word, the desires of our heart, richly all things to enjoy. That means we should enjoy the things that God has given us, and not let someone make us feel guilty about the things that we have. Never put the things ahead of God, but always give a good report, for what God has blessed you with, and what you have, because you did not do it, or get it yourself. In the early years of my life, I have been without, and I didn't know where it was going to come from, or how I was going to get it. Now I am in position where I have, and I can share and give to others, who don't have, and don't know where it's going to come from. So I enjoy giving to help the needy, and I'm going to enjoy the things that God has bless my wife and I with, and we are not going to feel bad about having things. Is not bragging, but the jealous can call it bragging if they like, and it won't bother us. Jesus said go tell your friends what great things that the Lord has done for you. So, when I share things that God has done for my wife and I, we are only doing what Jesus told us to do, to go give a good report. Pastors, and church leaders, and the readers of this book, go give a good report, of what great things, the Lord has done for you, and it will bless others to hear it!

Did I receive this so-called spiritual connotation that she gave me, in this email? No, not at all! This was not from God, this was all from her flesh, and I can back that up with audio recordings of her past abusive talking, and criticizing me and my wife accomplishments. So, readers why did I bring this up? I brought this up so that you should be aware of who's so-called trying to prophesy over you, or who is trying to speak something into your life that is not true. This came from the mouth of my former pastor's wife, who I have been with for thirty-four years. She admitted in time past, that she held some things against me, and was not the leader to me that she should have been, but never apologizing, and to this day has not apologized for that. Knowing that, why would I accept this so-called, spiritual connotation from her? I wouldn't, and I don't. **Proverbs 12:19** says, *"The lip of truth shall be established for ever: but a lying tongue is but for a moment."* When someone speaks the truth, God said it will be forever and ever, but when someone speaks a lie, it will only be for just a little while. **Isaiah 55:7** says, *"Let the wicked forsake his way, and the unrighteous man his thoughts: and let him return unto the LORD, and he will have mercy upon him; and to our God, for he will abundantly pardon."* **Jeremiah 17:9-10** says, *"The heart is deceitful above all things, and desperately wicked: who can know it? I the Lord search the heart... ."* The LORD knows the heart of everyone, and He said the heart is deceitful. The word **deceitful** means, *"misleading, or fraudulent."* So, the LORD is saying, the heart is misleading, and fraudulent above all things, and is desperately wicked, and that's why it's so easy for people to fabricate, embellish things, and lie. There are those who will lie on others to cover their own sins, or to make themselves look good, and others to look bad. Readers, <u>do you know what is worse than telling a lie</u>? **It is spending your whole life trying to cover or be true to the lie that you've told**. Lying is a choice, so readers, I challenge you to stop yourself in the middle of your lie, because change begins with you. **Proverbs 6:16** says, "*...seven things the LORD hate...,*" and one of those are in verse 17, "*...a lying tongue.*" (The Living Bible says, **"lying"**). I love The Living Bible translation because it says **lying** vs **a lying tongue**. A lying tongue only hits what comes out your mouth, but lying, hits the way you live your life, not only your words, but your lifestyle, and your deeds. Many people are living a lie, they never say anything with their mouth but their lifestyle is a lie, and God hates it, and if God hates it, we should too! Love the person, but hate the lie. Pastors and future leaders, I challenge you, don't be a liar in your words or deeds. **Numbers 32:23** says, "*...be sure your sin will find you out.*" God is giving you the opportunity to stop lying, He is giving you the space to repent, just as He did Jezebel, but unfortunately, she did not repent, because she believe she was doing no wrong. That is the modern-day Pharisee, in this day and time, everyone else around you is wrong, and you're the only one that's right. One day God will deal with your lying tongue, because according to **Proverbs 6:19**, God hates *"a false witness that speaketh lies... ."* God hates it when someone speaks falsely against, or about someone, and He also hates it when someone lies on others, because lying is a choice. You know whether or not someone is speaking something that's false and untrue into your life, don't let it happen. You say out of your mouth, just as I did, I don't receive that in the name of Jesus, because so shall your words be, that goes forth out of your mouth. When God has told you something, or have shown you something you hold onto it regardless of who's trying to prophesy or speak something over you that is contrary to what God has already told you. God is not a man that He should lie or repent, meaning, He does not change whatever He told you in the beginning, He will not come back later, or even years later, and change it through someone else. You have to learn to stand in the space that God has created for you, and not let someone come in so-called prophesy over you, and invade your space, and get you off the course that God has prepared for you.

Listen to this in **1 Kings 13:4-26** it says, *"And it came to pass, when king Jeroboam heard the saying of the man of God, which had cried against the altar in Bethel, that he put forth his hand from the altar, saying, Lay hold on him. And his hand, which he put forth against him, dried up, so that he could not pull it in again to him. The altar also was rent, and the ashes poured out from the altar, according to the sign which the man of God had given by the word of the Lord. And the king answered and said unto the man of God, Entreat now the face of the Lord thy God, and pray for me, that my hand may be restored me again. And the man of God besought the Lord, and the king's hand was restored him again, and became as it was before. And the king said unto the man of God, Come home with me, and refresh thyself, and I will give thee a reward. And the man of God said unto the king, If thou wilt give me half thine house, I will not go in with thee, neither will I eat bread nor drink water in this place: For so was it charged me by the word of the Lord, saying, Eat* no bread, nor drink water, nor turn again by the same way that thou camest. So he went another way, and returned not by the way that he came to Bethel. Now there dwelt an old prophet in Bethel; and his sons came and told him all the works that the man of God had done that day in Bethel: the words which he had spoken unto the king, them they told also to their father. And their father said unto them, What way went he? For his sons had seen what way the man of God went, which came from Judah. And he said unto his sons, Saddle me the ass. So they saddled him the ass: and he rode thereon, And went after the man of God, and found him sitting under an oak: and he said unto him, Art thou the man of God that camest from Judah? And he said, I am. Then he said unto him, Come home with me, and eat bread. And he said, I may not return with thee, nor go in with thee: neither will I eat bread nor drink water with thee in this place: For it was said to me by the word of the Lord, Thou shalt eat no bread nor drink water there, nor turn again to go by the way that thou camest. **He said unto him, I am a prophet also as thou art; and an angel spake unto me by the word of the Lord, saying, Bring him back with thee into thine house, that he may eat bread and drink water. <u>But he lied unto him</u>.** So he went back with him, and did eat bread in his house, and drank water. And it came to pass, as they sat at the table, <u>that the word of the Lord came unto the prophet that brought him back</u>: And he cried unto the man of God that came from Judah, saying, Thus saith the Lord, Forasmuch as thou hast disobeyed the mouth of *the Lord, and hast not kept the commandment which the Lord thy God commanded thee, But camest back, and hast eaten bread and drunk water in the place, of the which the Lord did say to thee, Eat no bread, and drink no water; thy carcase shall not come unto the sepulchre of thy fathers. And it came to pass, after he had eaten bread, and after he had drunk, that he saddled for him the ass, to wit,* **for the prophet whom he had brought back**. *And when he was gone, a lion met him by the way, and slew him: and his carcase was cast in the way, and the ass stood by it, the lion also stood by the carcase. And, behold, men passed by, and saw the carcase cast in the way, and the lion standing by the carcase: and they came and told it in the city where the old prophet dwelt. And when the prophet that brought him back from the way heard thereof, he said,* **It is the man of God, who was disobedient unto the word of the Lord**: *therefore the Lord hath delivered him unto the lion, which hath torn him, and slain him, according to the word of the Lord, which he spake unto him."*

Did you hear what the old Prophet said here at the end of the scripture, *"it is the man of God that disobey the word of the Lord."* **He did it!** He caused the man of God from Judah, to be disobedient to the word of the Lord, **by lying to him**. Not prophesying, **but a lying prophet**. Here's the man of God, the prophet, minding his own business, doing what God has told him to do. Now after he had completed the task that God had given him, God tells him, eat no bread, or drink no water, in this place, do not return the same way, but go another way. Now that's what God told him, and that's what he did, until the old prophet in the city heard about the good works this man of God did. The old prophet wanted to be part of it. He wanted to rub elbows or be a friend to this prophet, because he wanted to be close to him, but really he wanted to be seen as part of the good works that the man of God from Judah did. I have seen too many pastors today running behind the big name pastors, trying to be like them, or trying to be seen with them as part of the good works that they are doing, just like this old prophet. Pastors God called you because of what is in you, there is something special that God saw in you, He did not call you to try and be like someone else. So stop trying to be like someone else! You are not them, you are you, so be you! You don't know what that pastor, has gone through to get to where they are today. You have not paid your dues yet, you have not been found faithful yet over what you have, like the finances that comes into your ministry, or like the fifty members, or the one hundred members, or two hundred members, or even the five thousand members, or so on, that you have. You have not been found faithful over what you have. Jesus said in **Luke 16:10, & 12** *"He that is faithful in that which is least is faithful also in much: and he that is unjust (or unfaithful), in the least (or little), is unjust (or unfaithful), also in much..., And if ye have not been faithful in that which is another man's, who shall give you that which is your own?"* Jesus says here if you haven't done the right thing with the little that you have, who will give you increase? Or if you have not done the right thing with that which is someone else's, who's going to give you that which will be yours? If you have not done the right thing with that which belongs to someone else, like your ministry, or the finances that comes in to your ministry, none of these things belong to you, it all belongs to Jesus, and **He says, who should give you that of your own, Jesus is saying, <u>I'm not</u>!** Stop trying to force the hand of God to make your ministry be what you want it to be, because this is what the Pharisee did. The Pharisee did things that benefited, and pleased themselves. Listen to what Jesus has to say about them in **Luke 16:14-15** *"And the Pharisees also, who were covetous, heard all these things: and they derided him. And he said unto them, Ye are they which justify yourselves before men; but God knoweth your hearts: for that which is highly esteemed among men is abomination in the sight of God."* Now, look at what the Pharisees did when they heard what Jesus said in **Luke 16,** they <u>derided</u> Him. **Derided** means, *"to laugh at in scorn or contempt; or to mock."* Remember what I told you about the modern-day Pharisee early in this book, they are all about themselves, and no one else. When they hear the truth, and it pertains to them, they rejects it. That's what the modern-day Pharisee do in this day and time, they hear the truth about themselves, what they're doing or not doing and they rejects it. But Jesus said *"God knows their heart."* So, no matter how much you try and hide it, God knows your heart, and He said it is *"misleading, and fraudulent,"* and He can't allow you to prosper or be successful in what you do. You have to learn to seek God first, and not last. Stop seeking after people, for validation in what you are doing, or in your ministry, like this old prophet did. Jesus said in **Matthew 6:33** *"But seek ye first the kingdom of God, and his righteousness; and all these things shall be added unto you."* Pastors and church leaders if we would learn to seek after God, and his way of doing things, and not after people, Jesus said all these things that you desire will be added onto you. If you learn to seek God, and not man, all that you do in ministry will be very successful.

So the old prophet runs behind the prophet, seeking the man of God that came from Judah to be a part of the good works that this man did. The old prophet catches up with him, and find him sitting under an oak, minding his own business. Then the old prophet, prophesies to him and say hey man, we both preachers, I'm a prophet as you are, and God told me to tell you to come home with me and eat bread and drink water. Beware leaders, the devil will use anyone no matter what their title is to get you off the course that the Lord has prepared for you. You think your pastor won't lie, just let him or her get caught doing something they didn't have any business doing, or let their paycheck be on the line, or let someone point out to them, what they are doing is not right, they will lie in a minute, and put the blame off on someone else. Remember what God told the prophet? *"Eat no bread or drink no water in this place."* Do you remember what you read earlier in this book in chapter four, the three things that God told me to do while building the new church building? One of those three things was *"take no speaking engagement while building this building."* Do you remember what happened when I disobeyed? All the work stopped, money stopped coming in, six members left, and we had no more favor, until I repented and got it right. When God tells you to do something he is telling you to do, or not to do it for your own good, because he knows the ending from the beginning. Pastors, and church leaders, God is not going to change what He told you to do through someone else. **Malachi 3:6** says, *"For I am the Lord I change not...,"* and **Hebrews 13:8** says, *"Jesus Christ the same yesterday, and to day, and for ever."* God doesn't change like man changes. Whatever God told you to do, is what God wants you to do, and it might take years before God says now go do it. Don't let someone come and prophesy to you, telling you that God has changed, He is doing a new thing, and this is what God wants you to do now, don't fall for it. So, after the man of God, the prophet had gone home with him, and has eaten and drink water in the place, where God told him not to, and now God is going to use the mouth of the old prophet, **the same man that lied to him earlier, to now speak the truth**. He tells the prophet, the man of God, that the Lord said, because you have disobeyed the Word of the Lord, and have eaten bread, and drank water in this place, where he told you not to, you shall die. This is why I say to you leaders, you better know the character of the person that's trying to speak something over you or into your life. **1 John 4:1** says, *"Beloved, believe not every spirit, **but try the spirits** whether they are of God: because many false prophets are gone out into the world."*

There was a well-known pastor of a megachurch in Atlanta Georgia, some years ago, that allowed a man to come into his church and prophesy over him. This prophet had the pastor to sit in a chair and had four men to pick him up, and walk around the platform with him sitting in his chair before the congregation while he continued to prophesy over him. This man of God that was the prophet, what he was doing was an abomination to God, **and the pastor of the church allowed it**. He was lifting this pastor up before people. No man or woman should ever allow him or herself to be physically, spiritually or symbolically lifted up before man. Jesus Christ is the only one that should ever be lifted up before man. The pastor of this megachurch died a premature death within two years from the time that he allowed himself to sit in that chair and be lifted up before man. He had the choice to say, no, you will not lift me up physically, spiritually or symbolically before man, put me down! You don't just go with what someone say over you, or tell you to do, because you are the one that will pay the price in the end for your disobedient. Just like the prophet that came from Judah that we just read about in the scriptures, he died a premature death, because he listen to someone else, that changed what God told him to do in the first place. God will never change what he told you to do, through someone else. Remember, I told you earlier in this book in chapter four, when we was building our new church building, and God told me three things to do, and one of those things was to *"give like I've never given before."* I told you that I told other pastors how we were giving, and they said we shouldn't do that, you should keep that money to help with your building project. If I had a listen to them, and had done that, I would have disobeyed God, and brought death to the vision of building the new building debt-free. Pastors, you better know who you have coming into your church, call themselves, prophesying over you and your flock.

Now let me go back and say this concerning the prophecy that was spoken over me. I don't have a problem with walking away from this church building or letting go of anything that God has blessed me with, because they are only things. But I'm not going to listen to someone who is so-called prophesying over me, saying the Lord said, when I know the character of that type of person, and they are all about themselves, and they operate with pride, jealousy, lying and envy. I'm not saying she's not a prophetess, because that's not my place to judge, because we see in this scripture that we just read, that the old prophet lied, then God used the mouth of the same old prophet that lied, to now, tell the truth.

You need to be careful who's laying hands on you, and speaking over you, because a person say what they know, but they impart to you what they are. When you allow someone to speak over you, or lay hands on you, they are imparting into you the very essence of what they are, whether it's good or evil. Words are power and words our spirit, and they are life. Remember what Jesus said in **John 6:63** *"the words that I speak, they are* *spirit and their life."* When someone speaks over you, they're not just transferring information. They are transferring spirit, but whose spirit is being transferred, God or satan? A pure vessel releases purity, a perverted vessel releases, perversion. You are not just receiving words, you're receiving an importation of the essence of the speaker. Importation is more than just a transfer or a transaction of information. Remember, in **2 Kings 2:9** it says, that Elisha didn't just ask for Elijah's insight of things, he asked for a double portion of Elijah's spirit. In **Numbers 11:17** God took the spirit that was on Moses and he put it upon the 70 elders. So a spiritual transfer is very real and it's not just what a person says that you receive, it's what they carry. When someone lays hands on you or speak over you, they are imparting their character, their spirit, their grace *(and it could be God's grace or satanic grace)*, their mindset, and their spiritual condition. That's why **1 Timothy 5:22** says, *"Lay hands suddenly on no man, neither be a partaker of other men's sins: keep yourself pure."* God is warning you about the laying on of hands on others, and you allowing others to lay hands on you, and to speak over you, because importation is irreversible whether it be good or evil. Satan uses importation to accomplish his purpose. Just as God transfers the anointing, satan has a mindset that can be transferred to you. Remember in **Galatians 3:1**, Paul asked the question, *"O foolish Galatians, who has bewitched you."* A person can speak a word that plants doubt, fear, rebellion confusion, perversion, lust, and distraction into your spirit, and some words that is spoken, truly sound like prophecy, but they are the spirit of divination. Some words even sound like wisdom, but they are words of witchcraft. Who is praying over you, and who is prophesying over you? You've got to develop God's insight to be able to discern before you receive what someone is speaking over you. **Matthew 7:16** Jesus said, *"you shall know them by their fruits."* By the fruits that a person produce, you will know, who, or what, is true, or false." Don't just listen to what a person say, watch the fruits of a person's life, because when they lay hands on you, and speak over you, they are also speaking into you. **Jeremiah 29:9** says, *"For they prophesy falsely unto you in my name: I have not sent them, saith the Lord."* Notice what God says in this verse, anyone that gets up, and called themselves prophesying, but doing it falsely in His name, God said I didn't send them, they are a pretender, a false prophet, and you need to be aware of that. Again, I'm not going to say she's not a prophetess, but you better know who speaking over you, and I know that was NOT from God. I turned sixty-eight years old in May of this year, 2025, and I have been pastoring for twenty-eight years as of September this same year. I believe I have fought a good fight, and have kept the faith to do what God has called ME to do, so I don't have a problem with turning everything loose in God's appointed time to include this ministry, and not someone's else so-called appointed time. My wife and I are already grooming, preparing, training and teaching one of our children that has a pastoral call on their life to take over this ministry, that's how I know that what is written in this email is not of God, because I have no problem, and I say again no problem with turning all of this loose. **God knows what my wife and I have been doing for at least four years now, preparing this ministry for its next leader to take over.** I've watched pastors for over thirty-four years making ministry all about themselves, when they should be training someone else to take over their job, and they're not. Pastors, you will not live forever, and if you die without a successor, someone to take over your job, you have failed as a leader. Your job is to be **_mentoring_** someone to be your successor, like my wife and I are doing. That's why I know that this email is not of God. If I change, and do anything opposite of what God has already told me to do from the beginning, I will bring destruction to the vision of this ministry. If God wants me to change anything, He will speak to me personally, and not through someone else, just as he spoke to me from the beginning. Now, I will say this, God may speak through someone else to confirm what He has already spoke to you about. It will only be confirmation, **NOT A CHANGE**. God will not change what he told you to do from the beginning, because he knows the ending from the beginning, and he said, *"for I am the Lord, I change not."* I believe, the Lord is trying to get you to your destiny, but the devil will use other people and their title, to get you off the course that God has already prepared for you. Just like what the old prophet that came from Bethel, did to the man of God that came from Judah. We have to learn to stay the course, and not listen to the wrong people, no matter what, or what their title is!

Pastors and church leaders, you have to be tested before you get the things, to make sure that you will be faithful over the things, and not abuse the things, to include your ministry. We are always being tested, and I know I was tested before I even got the things that my wife and I have, to include this new church building. No one knows what kind of test, or what kind of things, or what kind of problems, you have had to endured to get where you are today, or to have the things that you have, but you and God. So, I was proven by God before I even got the things, so why would God tell me to give them up, when He's the one that blessed me with them in the first place for being obedient, He wouldn't. **1 Corinthians 4:2** says, *"moreover, it is required in stewards, that a man be found faithful."* I believe God found my wife and I faithful, years ago, and that's why he gave us the things, the desires of our heart. As long as we don't put the things ahead of God, why would he tell us to give them up? He wouldn't! Again, we don't have a problem with turning it all loose, if we know we're hearing from God. All this email is about, is to put me down, to try and make me look bad in the covenant, as though I'm bragging about what I have, and I can't turn it loose. Shame on you! All my former pastor's wife has done is made herself to look bad to this covenant on zoom, and through this email, and this book. It shows how she miss-uses her authority by lying, making up stories, embellishing things, and bullying people with her position as a prophetess, to get them to do what she want them to do, just as Jezebel did. This is what the modern-day Pharisee would do in this day and time, lie and put down others, to make them look bad, just to make themselves look good. God hates a lying tongue, and that's something you don't have to do. You will be judge for your lying tongue, because according to **Proverbs 6:16-19**, lying is one of the seven things that God hates. If God hate something, that means there will be a price to pay for doing what He hates. One thing I don't do is lie, because that's one thing I can control. Remember I brought out in chapter three, how I expose myself about my wrongness, and didn't lie about it. Yes I could have hidden my wrongness and lied about it and just exposed and talked about others and they're wrongness in this book. But as I stated earlier, if I had done that, that would make me a hypocrite, because that's what the modern-day Pharisee do today. They hide their own mess, but expose others when they are wrong. As a pastor I have always stood for what is right even a great personal cost, even when this is difficult. When you failed to stand for what is right you are lying. You can lie without even opening your mouth. You can lie by your action or a lack of action, and you lie by your lifestyle. If you break your word or break your promise, you are worse than an infidel, and that makes you a liar. One thing you can do, is keep your word. If your word fails, that means you have failed. If your word is no good, that means you're no good. You know why? Because you cannot separate you from your word. Your word is you and you are your word. Don't you know God knows when you don't keep your word. Don't you know that God knows when you break your word and not keep it, by being the pastor that you said that you would be to those people when they join your church, ministry or covenant, and you failed to shepherd them. Instead, you ran them off by lying on them, or you got upset with them and refuse to shepherd them and asked them to leave, like you did my wife and I, shame on you pastors, for doing that. **Like I said before, my former pastors turn into someone that I can't recognize anymore, <u>they turned into liars</u>**. When someone lie on you, there are three that know you're lying. **1.** The person that's telling the lie, know they're lying. **2.** The person that's being lied on, know that person is lying. and **3.** God Almighty know you are lying. The people around you that's hearing the story, don't know it's a lie. They're going along with it because they think they know you and they don't take you to be a liar, because you are their pastor, when in fact you are lying, and God knows it. The bible says in **2 Thessalonians 2:3**, *"Let no man deceive you by any means..."*, and in **Galatians 6:7** it says, *"be not deceived,"* and Jesus said in **Matthew 24:4, 11** *"...Take heed that no man deceive you. And many false prophets shall rise, <u>**and shall deceive many**</u>."* That means don't allow yourself to be deceived by others, because many false prophets, and prophetess are saying the Lord said, or the Lord showed me this, or that about you, **when it was NOT the Lord**. If there is a possibility that you can be deceived, then you need to take precaution that you are not deceived. Again as I stated earlier in this chapter, a **false** prophet or prophetess is an opportunitess, they wait and look for an opportunity to deceive others. Jesus said in **Mark 4:24** *"...Take heed **what** you hear... ."* And He goes on to say in **Luke 8:18** *"Take heed therefore **how** you hear... ."* Jesus is letting us know to be careful on *"what we hear,"* because people will lie, and He also tells us to *"take heed, how we hear,"* because people will embellish the story, and make it more than what it is. Be smarter than that, you have a responsibility not to allow yourself to be deceived, by listening to liars, or gossipers, because faith for anything comes by hearing. If you allow yourself to constantly hear the lies of liars, or gossip from gossipers, that thing will take root in your heart, and Jesus said in **Matthew 12:34** *"...out of the abundance of the heart the mouth speaketh."* Because you keep listening to them, you will now, start talking, and acting like them, and now you have allowed yourself to be deceived. **Cut them off, and don't listen to them!** As long as a liar or gossiper has an audience with an itching ear, that will listen to them, they will talk. I don't care what their title or position is, you have to cut them off, by telling them, I don't really care to hear it, and they will stop talking. Three types of people that I don't want around me, and I don't want to be around them, and that's a liar, thief, and a gossiper. Those three things are a choice, you choose to lie on someone, you choose to steal from someone, and you choose to gossip about someone, and that's your choice, but I don't have to be apart of it. You need to understand that the choices you make are long lasting, and forever life-changing, and there will be a price to pay for the choices you have made. There are always consequences for the choices that we make in life, whether they be good choices or bad choices. Good choices, bring good consequences, and bad choices will bring bad consequences. We all will pay a price for the choices we have made, because the Bible clearly says in **Galatians 6:7**, *"...we shall reap what we've sown."* A person that does not think about consequences before they say or do something is a person you cannot trust, because they are led by their own thinking. **Proverbs 14:12** and **Proverbs 16:25** both say the same thing, *"There is a way that seemeth right unto a man, but the end thereof are the ways of death (or destruction)."* They think that they are always right and their own thinking or actions, but it will lead to death or destruction. It doesn't matter who it is, what their title is, or what position they hold, they are untrustworthy, and I don't want to be around anyone that operate in these things. My prayer is always Lord remove them from my presence, or me from their presence. What more can you say or do, but pray for them, and others, and put them in God's hand. If you listen to me readers, I believe this will help you. Going through the things that my wife and I have gone through, one thing we have learned in thirty-four years of ministry is this, **there is nothing in life that is so bad, that something good couldn't come from it**. Always look for the good when you go through bad things. The good that I see and is taken with me from the experienced of being under my former pastors for thirty-four years is this. **Thirty-four years ago, God used my former pastor to**

place my feet on the straight and narrow path to bring me where I'm today. If God had not done that, I don't know where I would be today, but instead, God used him to put me on the course where I am today, <u>and that is good</u>, **and that is what I have taken with me from this experience**. My wife and I, hold nothing against our former pastors, and we love them with all of our heart. You might say, how can you love someone that has treated you in this way? Easy! When you have outgrown people, that means you have outgrown them even in your love walk, and that's what makes it easy. It becomes easy to walk in love when you know what the bible says about love. But if you are just **going through the motions of walking in love**, that's what makes it hard. A lot of christians just go through the motions and refuse to truly walk in love, because of what someone has done to them. **Isaiah 54:17** says, *"No weapon that is formed against thee shall prosper; and every tongue that shall rise against thee in judgment **thou** shalt condemn…."* There is nothing that devil can bring against you through others that will prosper against you when you are standing on what God has said. That means you have to condemn judgment when it comes against you, God has given you the authority to do that. Notice what God goes on to say in this verse, *"and every tongue that shall rise against **thee** in judgment **thou** shalt condemn."* **"Thou,"** means you, that means you have the authority to speak against it, and not wait on God to do it because He said, you shall condemn it. My wife and I have spoken against every judgment from others that has tried to come against us, and that it will not accomplish its purpose. That's how my wife and I did it, we have stood and will continue to stand on what God has said. Remember **Romans 8:31** says, *"What shall we then say to these things? If God be for us, who can be against us?"* When you have learned to walk in true love in spite of your feelings, that makes it easy. **1 Corinthians 13:2** says, *"...if I have not love, I am nothing."* God said, if we don't have love, we are nothing, but we know that we are the righteousness of God in Christ, and the love of Christ dwells within us, and that is what we must stand on. **1 Peter 4:8** says, *"And above all things have fervent love among yourselves: for love shall cover the multitude of sins or faults."* Love causes you to forgive others, and love covers all of our sins, and faults. **1 John 4:17** says, *"Herein is our love made perfect, that we may have boldness in the day of judgment: because **as he is, so are we in this world**."* This chapter says, *"God is love"*, and it gos on to say, *"as He is, so are we in this world."* If God is love, which He is, we are supposed to be love also, and not just in words, but in our deeds. That's how my wife and I could do it, and you can do it also by walking in love. It's very important that you know what love is, because you can't operate in something that you have no knowledge in. **Love** *is, "an outward expression of one's affection."* In other words, it's what's in your heart, it is an outward expression of what's in your heart. **Proverbs 23:7** says, *"for as a man thinketh in his heart, so is he."* When someone does you wrong, do you have love for them in your heart, or do you have hatred? Or are you plotting how you are going to get back at them? The New International Version bible says, in **1 Peter 3:8-9**, *"Finally, all of you, be like-minded, be sympathetic, love one another, be compassionate and humble. Do not repay evil with evil or insult with insult. On the contrary, repay evil with blessing... ."* One thing I've learned over the years is, you have to learn to be kind to unkind people, because they need it the most, and that's what love does. Never allow anyone to pull you down so low that you hate them, because hate is the opposite of love. Remember, the Bible says, *"love covers the multitude of sins or fault."* Do you truly walk in love? Can you truly show love to people even when they have done you wrong? **1 Corinthians 11:31** God said, *"...for if we would judge ourselves, we should not be judged."* Judge yourself to see what is truly in your heart, or are you truly walking in love, or are you just going through the motions in front of people, but behind closed doors you are something totally different. What is truly in your heart, **Matthew 12:34** Jesus said, *"...for out of the abundance of the heart the mouth speaketh."* What is coming out of your mouth behind closed doors, in secret? What is your action showing, love, or hatred? Whatever it is, God sees it, and knows it. **John 13:34** Jesus said, *"A new commandment I give to you. That you love one another; as I have loved you, that you also love one another."* Jesus is not telling us if we can work it into our busy schedule to walk in love. He is commanding us to walk in love. This is the last commandment that Jesus gave us. If we would learn to walk in love, there will be less crime and violence in the world. Everyone of us has the ability to walk in love, we just refuse to do so, and that's because of your flesh and you're unwillingness to change your way of thinking. Things are not going to happen by themselves, God has to have someone that he could work His principles through. The only thing that happens by itself is failure, you don't have to do anything to fail, just do nothing, and you will fail, but to be successful it requires something of you. It requires a can-do attitude and willingness to obey God. I'm going to quote **Dr. Martin Luther King Jr.** He said,*"Man must evolve from all human conflict, a method which rejects revenge, aggression and retaliation. The foundation of such a method is love."* That's powerful, and that's easy. He said, to **"evolve,"** which means *to develop ourselves*, that means *to change your way of thinking*, and and if we do that, we will get rid of revenge, aggression and retaliation, simply by walking in love. **Wise men said: "Don't seek revenge. The rotten fruits will fall by themselves."** See, you don't have to do anything to get back at people that has wronged you. If they're rotten to the core, they will fall by themselves to include their ministry. That's how my wife and I did it, we just walked in love. We wish nothing bad to happen to our former pastors and others, we just pray for them. **Romans 12:19** God said, *"...for it is written, Vengeance is mine; I will repay, saith the Lord."* That's a promise from God. So, let God handle them, is that so hard to do? Put the people that has wronged you in Gods hand, we are here to love the people in spite of their shortcomings. **1 Corinthians 13:13** says, *"And now abide, faith, hope, charity, these three; but the* *greatest of these is love."* Why do you think God said in this verse, but the greatest of these is love. I'll tell you why, it's because **LOVE** covers all of our faults, all of our shortcomings, anything that we've done wrong, love covers the multitude of sins or faults.

Ok, back to our covenant:
We were all made to sign a one-sided covenant agreement, IF we wanted to be under my former pastors as a covering, you must sign this whether you agree or disagree with it. Now, mind you, I had already been with my former pastor for twelve years at the time they wanted us to sign this covenant agreement. To make a long story short everyone in the covenant signed it. I was the only one to question it, before I signed it. When your leader wants you to do something that you disagree with, my former pastor's wife would say something like, *that's what the Lord showed me about you pastor Jake, you are very quick to disagree, <u>and the Lord said He hates that about you</u>*. **They have to make it sound spiritual, so they put it on the Lord, to try and get you to do what they want you to do**. What is this book about? The Modern-Day Pharisees: The Uncovering, who will try to force their will upon others, to get you to do what they want you to do. I told her no, I'm not in disagreement, I just have questions. As I said before, you better know who is trying to speak something into your life, or trying to get you to do something that you are not comfortable with in your spirit, so you better not do it, or accept it, because in the end, you will be the one that pay the

price for it. **Remember the story in 1 Kings 13th chapter that we just discussed about the old prophet that came from Bethel, who lied to the other prophet that came from Judah, and you saw in that, who paid the price**. It was the man of God, the prophet that came from Judah, that God told specifically what not to do. God told him, *"eat no bread, nor drink no water, in this place, but return another way."* You will pay a price for disobeying God when he tell you to do something, and you allow someone else to come to you and change what God has already told you to do.

Overtime, the way we all were being treated, everyone left the covenant except for two of us pastors. I tried to tell my former pastor and his wife why the pastors and people were leaving but, they didn't want to hear it. I brought up things to my former pastors that they were doing, and not doing, and also, not leading by example, but they could not receive that from me. Remember what I brought out earlier in chapter six, what Jesus said in **Luke 7:30** *"But the Pharisees and lawyers rejected the counsel of God against themselves... ."* Notice how the Pharisees rejected wise counsel that Jesus gave them, **against themselves, believing that they've done no wrong**. This is what the modern-day Pharisee is all about in this day and time, they can do no wrong, even when everything says, and shows, that you are wrong. The same thing still goes on today, with pastors, and leaders, rejecting council from others when they are wrong, but yet believing they've done no wrong.

On July 3, 2023, my former pastor and his wife told my wife and I, that we were dismissed from the covenant, we will not be your pastors any longer. After twenty-three years of the existence of the CCM covenant Agreement, and thirty-four years in ministry, and twenty-six years of pastoring, under my former pastors, my wife, and I, was told we were dismissed from the covenant, leaving only one pastor in the covenant out of fourteen of us. I have to say it this way, that was not good leadership, because you didn't want to hear about your wrongness as a leader but put all the blame on the people that left, and you done no wrong. Like I said earlier, the success or failure of a team or covenant always fall back to the leader. What I did not like about our covenant is, there was no transparency from our leaders. Everyone else is wrong, but they never do any wrong. You try and talk to the pastors about their wrongness, and they will deflect, by fabricating things on you, they will lie on you, they will make up stories about you, and will embellish those stories about you to others to make you look bad. All of this is done to get the attention off of themselves, and to get you upset, so you will leave the church so they can keep doing their deals in secret. If they cannot get you to leave the church on your own, they will eventually put you out, like they did my wife and me, and then lie to others, that you left on your own, because you're not there to defend yourself. But what are we reading about in this book? We are reading about, The Modern-Day Pharisees, The Uncovering, how God always have a way of uncovering your lies, and the things you have done.

Chapter 9: **Leaders That Answers To No One**

Remember, I told you that on 3 July 2023, my former pastors released my wife and I from under their authority. As soon as they released us from under them, we immediately, by the leading of the Holy Spirit got under someone else authority, that we can be accountable to. Apostles, prophets, evangelists, pastors and teachers that are under no one's authority, to be accountable to, and answers to no one, is a dangerous thing, and trouble will find you. Any pastor that is not under someone's authority, someone to answer to, is a person that is left to police themselves, and that is NOT accountability. Now, again, let me talk to you about the danger of absolute power, because you have no one to answer to, or no oversight. Absolute power will always lead to absolute abuse and corruption, because of no oversight. If you are a leader and especially a church leader that has no oversight, and are under no one's authority, or has no accountability, meaning you have no one to answer to or no one to keep you honest and on the straight and narrow, you will abuse your position, title, money, and people. If you have no oversight over you or you refuse to submit to the oversight that is over you, you are headed for a fall and great shall be your fall! Every pastor should be under someone's authority, if not, you can very easily get yourself into serious trouble. I said it before, and I'll say it again, God designed the system that we all be under someone's authority, someone to answer to.

Hebrews 13:17 says, *"Obey them that have the rule over you, and submit yourselves: for they watch for your souls, as they that must give account, that they may do it with joy, and not with grief: for that is unprofitable for you."* Notice what this verse says, *"obey them to have rule over you and submit,"* this is very clear, there is no misunderstanding this. God says two things here; number one He said **"obey"** which means **to do or carry out what someone says**. In order to carry that out, you must be under someone's authority. Number two He said **"submit"** which means **to accept or yield to a superior force, or to the authority or will of another person**. Again, in order to carry that out, you must be under someone's authority. This verse tells me that IF, and that is a BIG IF, you are truly call by God, we all must be under someone's authority, someone to submit to, someone to answer to, someone to help keep us on the straight and narrow. It's the same principal that God talks about in **Proverbs 29:15** where he says, *"...a child left to himself bringeth his mother to shame."* It's the same principal with a pastor that is not under anyone's authority, if he is left to himself, he shall bring his ministry, and himself to an open shame, by abusing his or her authority. What are we reading about in this book? We are reading about, the modern-day Pharisee, who does not submit to anyone's authority, but go about establishing their own righteousness. A pastor that is not under someone's authority, is one that goes about establishing his or her own righteousness. God requires us all to be under someone's authority. If

God created the ants to be under the authority of the queen ant, and He created the bees to be under the authority of the queen bee, what makes you think that it's ok with God that you are under no one's authority? God sees what the modern-day Pharisees are doing, and they will have their day in court. **2 Corinthians 5:10** says, *"For we must all appear before the judgment seat of Christ; that everyone may receive the things done in his body, according to that he hath done, whether it be good or bad."* **Ecclesiastes 12:14** says, *"For God shall bring every work into judgment, with every secret thing, whether it be good, or whether it be evil."* You can see in these two scriptures nothing shall be hidden everything shall be revealed. You will give an account whether it be good, bad, or evil, but you will give an account for your actions or a lack of action there of. I believe God gives every person the space to repent. That's why **Numbers 14:18** says, *"The LORD is longsuffering, and of great mercy... ."* He is waiting on you to repent and if you don't, I believe not only will you pay the price at the judgment seat of Christ, but you will pay a price before you leave this earth. I believe there will be a public fall, and the whole world will know and see what you have done because you refuse to own your wrongness. You will give an account for your actions in one place or another or maybe both. **Revelation 2:21** says, *"...that God gave Jezebel the space to repent, and she repented not."* God is waiting on you to repent of your wrongness, He is warning you everyday through other people's examples, look what happened to that man or woman, don't let it happen to you, repent! We are beginning to see prominent people in ministry fall every year: apostles, prophet, evangelist, pastors and teachers, because they have hidden their sins, and they refused to do the right thing and own it. Because of their responsibility, and accountability, over the lives of others, God could not allow them to continue in ministry. This is the modern-day Pharisee in this day and time, it is their desire to impose their will on another, even against that person's will. It is a shame when you have become so hard hearted that you can't even recognize when you are wrong. In the book of Romans, chapter 1, God refers to these type of people as having a reprobate mind. They know what is right, or the right thing to do, but yet refused to do it. **James 4 :17** says, *"Therefore to him that knoweth to do good, and doeth it not, to him it is sin."* Everyone around you have told you how wrong you are, but yet, you can't see it, and you refuse to change. Instead, you get people around you that are yes people, or man pleasers, to agree with you, to convince yourself, you are right in what you are doing, but great shall be your fall! I don't care what title you may have; no one is immune from the tricks of the devil. If the devil came and tested Jesus, what do you think he's going to do with us. So it's important that we guard our heart with all diligent against the tricks of the enemy.

For years, I have watched different pastors that are not under anyone authority, to include my former pastors, they would self-promote themselves giving themselves certain titles. Listen to what **Revelation 2:20** says, *"Notwithstanding*

I have a few things against thee, because thou sufferest that woman Jezebel, which calleth herself a prophetess, to teach... ." She was never God's choice to be a prophetess. God was against this woman, because she usurped her authority over her husband, and she self promoted herself, giving herself a title. The scripture says **"she called herself a prophetess."** She! Not God, but she! Called herself a prophetess. God never called her to be a prophetess. Now, notice what God says to the church of Ephesus in **Revelation 2:2** it says, *"I know thy works, and thy labour, and thy patience, and how thou canst not bear them which are evil: <u>and thou hast tried them</u>* **which say they are apostles, and are not, and hast found them liars."** Here's another case where God frowns, on self promotions. Here's a person that God talks about that was tried or tested, which called themselves an apostle, but was found to be a liar. God will let you do what you want to do, and He'll let you promote yourself, and call yourself whatever you want to call yourself, but in the end there's a price to pay, will God find you to be a liar. Do you remember after Judas betrayed Jesus, he went out and hung himself, and the disciples cast lots to choose the person to replace him as an apostle. The bible says in **Acts 1:26** it says, *"...the lot fell upon Matthias; and he was numbered with the eleven apostles."* Do you really think that would have been God's way to choose the next apostle, casting lots? I don't believe so, I don't believe Matthias was God's choice for the next apostle because, think about it, you never hear anything else about him from that day forward. I believe Paul was God's choice, and not Matthias, and if the disciples had of waited, I believe that God would've revealed it to them. Pastors and church leaders, too many times we get ahead of God when it comes to promotion, we want it now, we don't want to wait, but we must be tested, and then, and only then, God will reveal His choice for promotion. This sound like something that the modern-day Pharisee would do, self promote themselves. I believe if God is going to promote us, we must be tried and tested first under someone's authority, and God will use that person to promote us, after we have been found faithful.

In June 1989 according to my brother and his wife, that was attending my former pastor's church at that time, this was before I got saved, and became a member, said that my former pastor invited the pastor from Augusta Georgia to be a guest speaker and that he was supposed to ordain him while he was there. According to my brother, the ordination did not take place, and that pastor said openly, *I see some things in the spirit,* so he did not ordain him. Instead, he said I forgot to bring the ordination with me. Now, mine you my former pastor ordain me over the telephone from another country, and later mailed me my ordination, and when he visit my church in North Carolina at a later date, my former pastor laid hands on me and prayed for me at that time. Question, why couldn't the pastor, from Augusta Georgia do the same thing for my former pastor? I'll tell you why, again in the spirit he saw something in my former pastor that he didn't like that was not right. Leaders you have got to learn to stay put, until someone find you faithful enough to ordain or promote you. It's not about you, it's about God, and whom He wants to use, for his purpose, we're just the vessel that He will use when he is ready. So, stop being selfish, one thing I learned over the years, is that God didn't put us here as a part of the five-fold ministry to get a pat on the back or to say, well done or at-a-boy. He put us here so that he could be here Himself through us. You are not here for yourself, you are here so that God can make his presence known to His people, through you. Let's get it straight and remember why we're here. You're here because God saw something in you that he can make his present known through you. I think somewhere we have lost focus, and lost the ability to discern, to see, to know, to understand, what our purpose is. We think if God can't do it through us, it can't get done because He can't use anyone else, but me. Pastors, you have gotten so self-righteous that you think that you are it, I am all God need, He don't need anyone else, but me. Your attitude is, I am God's right hand man, a woman, and all He needs is me. You think that you're the only person God can use, you are the only one that can get the work done for God. Pastors! Who are you to have such a self-righteous attitude, to think that you are the only one that God can use! God can use whom soever He may choose, and you have no say so in the matter. You say, I'm working for the Lord and I'm pushing fourth, and advancing the kingdom for the Lord. We are not working for the Lord. **2 Corinthians 6 :1** says, *"We then, as workers **together** with him….."* We are working together with Him, not for Him.

He's allowing us to work with Him, but in all things, we have to be proven, if we're going to work with Him. You act like God need you! If God can create the universe without your help, why does He need you now? He doesn't! Jesus is the head of the church, and He is allowing us to work with Him, not for Him. What I must understand is, what's my place with Him. Pastors, if we are going to work with Him, then we need to educate ourselves, so when we do what we do we know that we're not breaking the law out of ignorance, because ignorance of the law is no excuse. Case in point:

According to court documents, here's a pastor in Sanford, North Carolina, just down the road, not far from my church, facing charges and up to ten years in federal prison for Medicare fraud. **A pastor! Out of all people! A pastor!** As I stated before, no, you don't need a college degree to preach, the gospel, but I tell you what a college degree will do, it will teach you about Introduction to Business, Business Law I and II, and IRS Laws, and it will help keep you out of trouble. My wife and I took these courses when we were in college, and they have definitely been a big help for us in ministry. Court documents state, "this pastor in Sanford, North Carolina, is also the Director of a church affiliated organization to help the needy. Court document state, that he pled guilty to Medicare fraud charges. He said his intention was to help people, and he didn't know that he was doing anything illegal. Now he stated he didn't know he was doing anything illegal, but yet he received more than $10,000 in kickbacks and bribes all part of a Medicare fraud scheme. He received kickback payments in exchange for the referral of his church members names as patients for a physician, using them saying they did cancer tests, but they never did. Those names were submitted to Medicare for reimbursement that was never done." Now, you might say what's wrong with that, and what's illegal about that? It becomes illegal when you're submitting those names to Medicare, but those people never received any type of test, and you filed the paperwork to Medicare for reimbursement, that makes it fraud. I believe that if this pastor had taken, at least these four college courses, not necessary to get a degree, but being equipped with this knowledge, and information, it would've kept him out of trouble. Pastors sometimes we lose our way, listening to the wrong people. When you take kickback payments, and bribes, you know that you're doing something illegal. I believe if this pastor had been under someone to hold him accountable, this would have never happened. No matter what it is, breaking the law, treating people wrong, not walking in love, miss using church funds, being a bully, or abusive to God's people. No one have to tell you, you're wrong, you already know it, and the bible says, *"be sure your sin will find you out."* We are talking about The Modern-Day Pharisees: The Uncovering, how they are all about themselves, and you can see it plainly wherever you go.

Have you ever read about the story in First and Second Kings about a husband-and-wife name Ahab and Jezebel. Ahab was king and wanted to do the right thing, but he listened to his wife who usurped her authority over him and did evil things. The story says that Ahab wanted to buy this vineyard from another man, but this man didn't want to sell his vineyard, so Ahab went back home, laid down on his bed and was sad and would not eat, his wife came in and asked him why are you sad, why won't you eat? He said because the gentleman would not sell me his vineyard. She reminded him saying, you are the king, in other words she was saying you can just take the vineyard if he doesn't want to sell it. Ahab being king, didn't want to do that, he didn't want to abuse his authority as king, he wanted to do the right thing, and get the vineyard the right way. So, his wife Jezebel writes a letter in his name, and uses his seal, and send it to some other people about the man that own the vineyard. She concocted and fabricated a lie and told them to have two witnesses to lie on him and say that he has blaspheme God and the king. Take him out in stone him to death and let me know when it's done. They got the letter and falsely accuse the man of blaspheming, and they took the man out and stoned him the death. They told Jezebel and she told her husband, the man is now dead, and the vineyard is now yours. Now, if that's not evil, I don't know what it is. She had a man murdered, because he would not sell his own property. That's the modern-day Pharisee, you won't what you want, when you want it, and don't care how you get it. She is a queen, a leader, and a prophetess, she someone who won't do the right thing but lies to have a man killed. She is supposed to be a leader of the people, but instead, abusing her position, abusing her authority, abusing her title, and fabricating a story, just to take this man property to give to her husband. Believe it or not, it goes on today with the modern-day Pharisee, not physical death, but death to other people's careers, to other pastors ministries, death to what other people are doing. You are jealous of them, and what they have, you are jealous of what God has done for or through them. You lie and fabricate stories on them just to try and make them look bad, saying they always bragging about what they have, and you do this because you know that most people are quicker to believe a lie than the truth, just as Jezebel did. This is with the modern-day Pharisee is doing today, but under cover, and in secret, and it has to be uncovered. I know it happens, because it happened to my wife and I, but thank God that He's on our side. It didn't do any damage to our ministry, or to our character because if God be for you, who can be against you.

Let me tell you what happened to my wife and I, and how my former pastor's wife devised the plan to try and discredit us as confident pastors. Doing our Monday mornings teachings on zoom, my former pastor's wife finally devised the plan so she can come down on me not my wife but only me, because she couldn't control me. My former pastors operate this way, if they can't control you, then they'll devise a plan to get rid of you, and that is very poor leadership. They'll fabricate things on you to make you get upset, and leave the ministry on your own, but she couldn't do that to us. But if they can't get you to leave on your own, they will tell you to leave, saying we are not going to be your pastors any longer, because you don't follow instructions, which is a lie. Since we would not leave on our own, she came up with this plan that she'll have all us pastors to teach a 15-minute class on Monday mornings on zoom. As soon as she said that, the Holy Spirit said to me, pastor Williams **this is a set up,** to try to discredit you. She assigned each one of us pastors a class to teach. The Holy Spirit said to me, "pastor Williams, no matter how good you teach your class, it's not going to be good enough for her, because it's all part of her plan to get you mad enough to leave." To be honest, I really don't believe her husband knew anything about this plan that she came up with, she did this on her own, without his knowledge, just as Jezebel did. **Proverbs 19:21** says, *"There are many devices in a man's heart; Nevertheless the counsel of the LORD, that shall stand."* It is evil when you sit, and come up with devious plans, or devices just to try and discredit someone, or to get them mad enough, to leave the ministry, or to get back at them. **But truth will always prevail over a lie**. But doesn't this sound just like what Jezebel did in First Kings chapter 21, who schemed and came up with a plan to have a man kill to take his property. The reason why you do this as a leader, is because it's in your power to do it, and you think you can get away with it. Look at what God says in **Micah 2:1,** *"Woe to them that devise iniquity, and work evil upon their beds! when the morning is light, **they practise it, because it is in the power of their hand**"*. Now listen to how the Message Bible says this in **Micah 2:1,** *"Doom to those who plot evil, who go to bed, dreaming up crimes! As soon at it's* *morning, they're off, full of energy, **doing what they've planned**.*" In other words, God says you do it, because you think that you can get away with it, because of the authority that you have as a leader. Don't be deceived, you think you are getting away with it, but you're really not, because God said, **"Doom to those who plot evil."** God see you, and knows what is in your heart, and there will be a day of punishment. Now here go's my former pastor's wife, scheming, and coming up with a plan just to try to get me mad, an run me off, and that is very demonic. Now isn't that's what we are talking about in this book, how The Modern-Day Pharisees: The Uncovering, do their deals, and try to force their will and desires on others to have their way. I believe that this is what is in her heart, to try and discredit me, because I am outspoken, and I said she act like a bully. Pastors, and church leaders when you seek revenge, and carry it out through a devious plan, makes you a very poor leader. God knows what's in your heart, and He knows what you're doing, and what you are thinking of, even if your spouse doesn't. Look what Jesus says here in **Matthew 15:19-20** *"For out of the heart proceed **evil thoughts**..., He said, these are the things which defile a person... ."* What defiles a person? Jesus said, **"your evil thoughts,"** that's what defiles you, that's what makes you unclean in you're thinking. I said it before, and I'll say it again, it's demonic when you allow yourself to have evil thoughts on how you are going to get back at others, and then carry it out, that's not love. I believe it's the actions that we take against others that defines who we really are, because love would not cause us, or allow us to do the things that we do. It is a condition of the heart, out of it proceed evil thoughts, and plans. When you carry those thoughts, and plans out or even speak those thoughts out, is demonic. **2 Corinthians 10:5** says, *"Casting down imaginations, and every high thing that exalteth itself against the knowledge of God,* **and bringing into captivity <u>every thought</u>** *to the obedience of Christ."* You have to bring the thoughts into captivity, meaning under control. God is not going to do it for you, you have to do it. When the thought, and imaginations comes, you have to get rid of it immediately, by doing what **Philippians 4:8** says, *"Finally, brethren, whatsoever things are true, whatsoever things are honest, whatsoever things are just, whatsoever things are pure, whatsoever things are lovely, whatsoever things are of good report; if there be any virtue, and if there be any praise,* **<u>think on these things</u>**.*"* If you would think on these things when evil thoughts, or imaginations come up in your mind, you will not carry out devious plans to get back at someone. That's why God tells us to cast down thoughts, and imaginations. You know why He said, cast it down? If you let those thoughts stay there in your mind, they will eventually go down to your heart, and once it's abundance in your heart, your mouth is going to speak or you are going to carry out those thoughts, or plans. I believe a person that thinks this way really need to spend a lot more time in prayer and studying their bible. **Matthew 12:34-35** Jesus said, *"...for out of the abundance of the heart the mouth speaketh. A good man out of the good* *treasure of the heart bringeth forth good things:* **and an evil man out of the evil treasure bringeth forth evil things.**" A leader that carries out a devious plan like this, gave birth to it first in their mine, and then they let it get into their heart, and then carried it out, and that makes it a premeditated act. It's the condition of your heart. You thought about what you was going to do, and you had every opportunity not to do it, but instead, you carried it out, and that makes it demonic. Readers, what are we reading about in this book, we are reading about The Modern-Day Pharisees: The Uncovering, how is all about themselves being in control, and forcing their will, and desires upon others. The Holy Spirit had already showed me and warned me what was coming, so I was already prepared for it. Now mine you, my wife and I have been pastoring now for twenty-six years and I believe we have been very successful at it, and to teach a 15-minute class is nothing for us. The Holy Spirit showed me, that she can't attack me by myself, because it would look too obvious what she is doing. I told my wife this is what's going to happen, no matter how good I teach my class, it's not going to be good enough for her, no matter how good it was. Her plan was to attack mine and the other female pastor class, and say it's not good enough, that was really bad, but my wife and the other male pastor, class would be perfect. **<u>Now that's just pure evil</u>**. When you devise a plan in your heart like this, and carry it out, just to discredit someone, because you couldn't control them, is a premeditated act, and I say again, that's nothing but evil. **Proverbs 12:19** says, *"The lip of* *truth shall be established for ever: But a lying tongue is but for a moment."* When you know people will lie, are lying, just put them in God's hand, because there lying tongue is only going to be for a little while. Believe it or not, it was exactly what the Holy Spirit showed me would happen. The other female pastor, and her husband taught their class, and just as I said, his class was spot on perfect, but her class wasn't good enough, just as I said. My former pastor's wife came down on the young lady hard, right out in front of everyone on zoom. It was done in ways that should have never been as a leader, in a way that I really felt sorry for her. Later that day I called her to encourage her, because words of encouragement will go a long way. I told my wife, next Monday when I teach, watch it won't be good enough. The next week my wife and I taught our class, my wife's class was spot on, perfect, and my class was spot on perfect also, **at the time**, so I thought, because there were no negative comments. Everyone made their comments afterwards and gave positive feedback, **and that's not what my former pastor's wife wanted**. First, my former pastor said, **"this was good,"** and he went on to talk about how good it was. Then the other male pastor, gave his comment, and he said, **"pastor, you and your wife had to be hearing from God to put pastor Williams, and his wife together like that to teach their classes, because their classes complemented each other, that was good, this was really good"**. Then the other female pastor, gave her comment she talked about, **"how good the class was"**. Then my former pastor's wife made her comments and the first thing she said was, **"this was really good,"** and she went on to give more comments, because in front of everyone she had no choice, but to make a good comment. **Now that's what everyone said this week**. I just knew my former pastor's wife was going to talk about how bad my class was, but she didn't. So, I said to myself, maybe I missed God, when the Holy Spirit was speaking to me about what my former pastor's wife, was going to say, so I thought. Next week on Monday morning when we came on zoom the other two pastors wasn't on. It was just my wife and I and our former pastors. I believe my former pastor's wife told the other pastors not to come on zoom that Monday morning, because they needed to talk to me and my wife alone. **I believe she did that so that would be no other witnesses to dispute what she said <u>the previous week</u>, and no witnesses to what she's about to say**. When I saw that, I said to myself <u>here it comes</u>, it's going to be on, because there is no one to dispute her. Truly this is what happened, first thing my former pastor's wife said, **"your class was bad, you were all over the place, you didn't teach what we asked you to teach. You talked about what you told your people and that's not what we ask you to teach"**. I remain respectful and told her that's not what you said last week, and then I quoted to her exactly what she said, because I wrote everything down word for word, because I had recorded all of it. I wish I could play the recordings for you readers, just so you can hear what she said, and how she acted. So, to make a long story short, she went off on me and told me I was a liar, I don't care what you wrote down, she said, I didn't say those things, and then my former pastor said, no, she didn't say those things, I'm the one that said those things. He said, I said those things, because she got on me later for saying your class was good, when I knew that was not good. I said to my former pastor, no sir, you did not say those things, your wife said those things, because I wrote down with each person said. Now, that's very demonic and evil when you can manipulate your own husband to get him to believe, and say what you want him to say, but isn't that's the same thing that Jezebel did with her husband, Ahab? Yes, she usurped her authority over him, and manipulated him to be able to do what she wanted to do. I wanted to tell them so bad right there that I had recorded the whole thing, and I can play it for you, but I wouldn't do it because I wanted to be able to continue recording without interruptions. **That's the type of people that my former pastors have become, liars!** When they can't control you, and they can't fabricate enough things to make you quit the ministry on your own and leave the church they would keep trying until they find something that would work. **They really turned into people that I would have never imagined.** They used to be the type of people that if you heard these sorts of things about them, you would say no, not them! That can't be true, I can't believe that, and I won't believe that. But doesn't the scripture say in **Matthew 24:24,** that Satan has even blinded the mind and *"deceived even the very elect?"* When you have no one to answer to, or someone there to talk to you, to keep you straight, satan will feel your heart with all kinds of evil plans. When there is a void in your spiritual walk, satan will rush in to fill that void with his evil plans, just as he did with Jezebel. Satan filled her heart with an evil plan, so she fabricated a story to have a man killed, to take his vineyard. My former pastors will do everything they can to discredit you, or to make you look bad, when you don't agree with them, and then tell you to leave, because they can't control you, like they did my wife and me. **My former Pastor, and his wife used to be very good leaders, <u>I should know, I've been with them for thirty-four years</u>**. But somehow, or someway they went left and start operating with the Jezebel spirit. Let me say this about a Jezebel spirit, a Jezebel spirit can be a man or a woman. When we here of prostitution we always think of a woman, and we think sexual, but it does not just mean a woman, or sexual. You can prostitute yourself for favor with others, for positions, for power, for titles, as well as money. A Jezebel Spirit does not care about the truth. A Jezebel, just want total control. A Jezebel spirit uses false accusations to get what he or she wants. A Jezebel spirit will try to corrupt good people, and desire to destroy those, or the reputation of those that won't be corrupted. A Jezebel spirit is someone who won't repent even when they're told how wrong they are. A Jezebel spirit leaves a trail of broken and devastated relationships. A Jezebel spirit is a spirit of envy, pride, jealousy, deception, and condemnation. If you are a leader and are operating with these characteristics, you are operating with a Jezebel spirit, even though you think you're not, when is clearly seen by others that you are, and you need to repent. God knows your heart and he knows what you have been doing even though you have been good at hiding it from others. God is giving you the space to repent just as He did Jezebel, but it's up to you. It is really a foul spirit when you allow satan to invade your heart and do those kinds of things, you truly need to step down from your position, and spend more time with the Lord in prayer and meditating on His word until you get your heart right. When you are a pastor that answers to no one, you will allow satan to invade your heart this way, because of pride, and you think you are right in your actions. If you had a pastor over you, someone to answer to, someone that my wife and I would have been able to goto, and talk to about their actions, just maybe things would have turned out different, or better. This is the modern-day Pharisee in this day and time, how they do they work in secret and everything has to be their way. What a shame!

Pastors and future leaders, the only reason I brought these things out is so you can see how easy it is to abuse your authority or your position, even when talking with season pastors. Readers if you are a leader, there is no way you should have treated season pastors in this manner. These are pastors that has been pastoring for twenty-six years, and not someone that's just starting out as a young pastor. So, what if they have outgrown you, even in teaching, they are supposed to. I said it before, and I'll say it again, the road to opportunity through others, is often the road that is most overlooked by leaders, because they think God can only use them. You are supposed to be a mentor to them, and not someone that is always tearing them down. Don't put someone down just to try and make them look bad, and make yourself, look good, just because they have outgrown you. **Leaders that think this way, will always miss the opportunity, that is right in front of them**. Pastors and future pastors, we wonder why people leave our church, it's because of this type of leadership, which ought not to be. Now don't get me wrong, I know people leave churches for all kind of reasons, **but it should not be because of you being an abusive leader**. They are not your people, they are God's people, and they should be treated as such. Most of the time when people leave your church, it's because the person can't receive correction, or they don't want to hear the truth about themselves, or it's something that the pastor has said, or done. If you are going through these things, I encourage you be strong in the Lord, and in the power of His might and stay put. No matter how you are feeling, and it doesn't matter what you're going through, there is a purpose in it. You might say this can't be God, because no pastor is going to talk to, or treat anyone this way or do the things that he or she is doing that you have brought out in this book, and called themselves a Christian. Don't move, stay put and wait on the Lord, because God is perfecting you; He is growing you; He is developing you, and when you go through these things, it will mature you. Just remember, the Lord is always on the side of what is truth and right, and the truth always has a way of coming to the light. Just like writing this book, I believe I have done the right thing by writing about what you can learn from my experience in thirty-four years of ministry, **to help** pastors, future pastors, and church leaders, those that has an ear to hear, and a heart to receive. This book is to prevent them from falling in the same traps, pitfalls and continuing the cycle as other leaders. God has to have someone who is willing to stand for what is right. He hast to have someone that He can work and speak through to accomplish His purpose. God has and we'll continue to fight our battles regardless of what is said or done by others.

Chapter 10: Be A Better You

Pastors, and future leaders, just as I stated in chapter eight, a true leader invest in people by **_mentoring_** them. You don't invest in buildings, programs, conferences, or any other thing, only people, because a person is your successor, not a building, programs, or conferences. Legacy is what we leave behind. **Proverbs 13:22** says, *"A good man leaves an inheritance for his children's children...."* Meaning, a good man's life possessions is left to his grandchildren, and not someone else. A good successful leader leaves a legacy, **_a successor_**, someone to takeover from him or her, because there is no true success without a successor. Pastors, if you die without a successor, you have failed as a leader, because you should be mentoring someone else to take over your job. If you are doing your job by mentoring others, you should become insignificant, and your ministry should be able to function without you. Ministry is not all about you, it's about you leaving **_a successor_**, someone to carry on the work. As leaders we must learn to invest in people, so we will have a successor. So the question we must ask ourselves as leaders is this, what legacy are you leaving for the next generation, and do you have a successor? Pastors, I encourage you, be a better you, and invest in a successor, because they are the next generation of leaders.

Pastors, be a better you, be a better pastor to your pastors, leaders, and congregation members, then your pastor were to you. They might have done the best that they could do, for whatever reasons. Maybe it was because of a lack of leadership skills, or lack of education, or something else, I don't know, but you have to forgive them and walk in love, and be better yourself. Pastors, sometimes you have to put yourself in that person's shoes that you are talking to and see things the way that person see them. You will never understand people until you learn to see things from their perspective, and point of view. When you do that, then, and only then, will you understand why that person thinks the way they think, talk the way they talk, and act the way that they act. Only then will you be equipped with the right information, and now ready to witness to that person. I believe if more of us took the time to just listen to another person's perspective we would understand that, that person has a wound that can only be healed by the blood of the Lord Jesus Christ. Pastors, stop being jealous when someone out do you in ministry, we're in this together, **this is not a competition**. I don't understand why some pastors get jealous of other pastors and can't be happy for them, because they have done something better or greater than they've done. But that is the action of the modern-day Pharisee, it's all about themselves, and they will not be happy for others. Pastors, learn to be a better you, because God has designed the system so that the next generation, do better than the former generation. And the next generation that comes behind, that generation, due much better than, that former generation, and so on, and so on. That's how God has designed the system to work. Pastors, don't you expect your physical children to do better in life than you've done? You might have done very well in life yourself, but you still want your physical children to do better and greater things in their life, then you've done, you want them to be better, because they are the next generation. Well, that's the way that God has also designed the spiritual system to work in ministry. When my former pastor launched me out in 1997, in my own ministry, he should expect me to do bigger, better, and greater things than he has done, because I have now become the next generation of pastors. I should do better than he has done in ministry. Again, **it's not a competition**, is what my pastor, should expect of me, because that's how God has designed the system to work. My pastor might have done great in ministry, but me as the next generation, I am supposed to do far better and greater things than he has done, and I have. He should be proud of me, and what God has done through me, just as though you are proud of your own physical children doing better and greater things in life than you've done. Pastors, you should be the same way with your spiritual sons and daughters when they do greater and better things in ministry than you've done. Didn't Jesus say in **John 14:12** *"...the works that I do shall he do also; and **greater works** than these shall he do…."* You should expect that, because that's what Jesus said, **_greater works_** shall they do, so be a better you, and never envy them, and don't be jealous of what they've done, and please don't operate in pride, because they are supposed to do, **greater works** than you've done.

Pastors, be a better you, when you operate in envy, jealousy, and pride, is a sign that you are an immature, and insecure pastor. When you operate in these things, that is a sign of being insecure to what God has called you to be. An insecure pastor is a danger to the position, so I want to give you six signs that you may be, or you may have an insecure pastor, and you need to listen carefully because an insecure pastor, is a false prophet or prophetess main target. When a false prophet or prophetess find a weakness in your life, like being insecure, they will exploit it to manipulate you. Number 1: An insecure pastor answer to no one, yet they preach submission, but they themselves are under no one's authority. Number 2: They silence prophetic words that comes from others that challenge their comfort, and what they are doing, or doing in secret. Number 3: They offer little to, no guidance, no direction, and no mentorship. Number 4: They micromanage your spiritual life, and they always have a word from the Lord for you, but it is not a true word, it is a word to hold you back, because they see greatness in you, but they do not want you to outgrow them. Number 5: They constantly compete with other gifts and have need to put down or cast doubt on other who possess gifting that they may or may not have. Number 6: They need to control everything that God has to say by suppression or oppression, if it can't come through them, it can't be said.

Pastors, you need to be mindful and give attention to these six things that is going on in the church, because this is how the modern-day

Pharisee operate today, and they are doing it for self-gain.

Pastors just because you are called, does not mean you are ready, or sent yet. **Romans 10:15** says, *"And how shall they preach, except they be sent... ."* You need to be under authority, because revelation without restraints produces arrogance, or overbearing pride, and that is dangerous. So, can you see the need to submit to a process to mature you, so you can be a better you? I encourage you to wait on your time. If you started your ministry before you were ordained, you were not sent, you just got ahead of God and just went. Your covering must be chosen wisely, and God knows who is best for your development and growth because your destiny depends on it. So just maybe you need to wait on God, shut down, sit down, and get ordained under the right covering, and start over, and that is not a bad thing when you do that, it's being humble. Remember, you are the one that got ahead of God, and went before you were sent, and that is why your ministry is not what it could have been. So, I submit unto you, be a better you, and humble yourself and start over, and watch what God do in your ministry and life, exceedingly, abundantly above all that you can ask or think.

Pastors and future leaders, be a better you, the house of God has no place for politicians, doing and saying things to gain favor with people or they with you. God did not call you to be a politician, he called you to preach the gospel. According to **Jeremiah 3:15** we are called to *"feed the sheep* *and feed the lamb with **knowledge** and **understanding**,"* and not to teach or preach for our own political gain. And that's what the modern-day Pharisee do in this day and time, talk to the people in such a way just to gain their favor. God sees and knows your motive behind what you say and do, you may hide it from others, but you can't hide it from God. If you want to be a politician, then go run for public office somewhere, and leave the house of God to those that wants to do what God has called them to do, because politics has no place in the house of God.

When ever I launch out sons and daughters in their own ministry to pastor, I'm going to let them always know that I am proud of them, and pulling for them 100% that they do, bigger, better, and greater things than I have done. You should always be proud of your spiritual sons and daughters, no matter what, fail or succeed, because they are still, your spiritual, sons, and daughters. Whether your physical children's fail or succeed in life, they're still your children, and you love them in spite of. You're proud of them because they are your children and they've done their best, and so should you be with your spiritual sons, and daughters. Every spiritual son, and daughter must be proven, in order to go to the next level. It's just like in school, it's no different. Every child must complete the required curriculum and pass every test in order to go to the next grade, or to graduate. The principal is the same, it's no different in the church. Every leader must pass every test that is set before them, in order to go to the next level spiritually. The bible says in **1 Corinthians 4:2** *"moreover, it is required in stewards, that a man be found faithful."* That means your spiritual leader, must find you faithful, before they give you responsibility. You never know when the test, or what kind of test is coming, just be ready. You can't just declare yourself faithful, if so, we all would have done that. No, you must be tested, and found faithful.

Let me tell you a story about a young man that I had with me for twelve years. I new it was time for me to launch him out into his own ministry. In or about August 2018, I told him that in 2019, I'm going to launch him and his wife out into their own ministry, but out of fear he said he didn't feel as though he was ready. He asks, could he wait? I said it is understandable that you don't feel as though you are ready, but he asked me, could he wait until 2020? I said if that's what you want to do, I'll let you wait but I know you are ready, and I know the time is 2019, he said I'll wait till 2020. The Holy Spirit said to me, he must be tested. So, I tested him, this way. I told him to go out and start looking for a building, a place that you can start your church in. I said don't sign anything or pay for anything, just look for a place. I had to give him a way to be tested. Just like God did with Abraham. Abraham really really wanted a son, and when he finally got the son after seventy-five years, God told him to go and sacrifice him to Me. That was a test. So, the test for the young man, had to be something he really really wanted. **It would show me where his true heart was at**. True enough, this is what happened.

He went out and found a building that he could used to start his church in. The former church that had the building, left the sound equipment, and the chairs in there. It was nicely renovated, and nicely painted, all he really had to do was go in and get started. Now, his big test! He comes back to me, and said, pastor, I found a building and I know I said that I wanted to wait till 2020 before you launch me out into my own ministry, but I don't want this building to get away, I want to go now. I told him if it's truly God I don't care who come along, it's your building even if you have to wait till 2020. My wife told him just because you found the building is not the reason to change your mind now and say I want to go now. The Holy Spirit said to me this is the perfect thing to test him with. **"Tell him to wait."** To make a long story short. I said to him, no, I want you to wait until 2020 which you said you wanted to do. He said, *"well I kind of figured you were going to say that, so my wife and I, we're going to go forward anyway."* I said OK, if that's what you want to do, I just can't be a part of it. I said who is going to license and ordain you? He told me don't worry about that, I got that taken care of. I told him, we all must be tested before God will send us forward to represent him, and I told him, you never know how the test is going to come, and you just failed the test. By me telling you no, I want you to wait, and you said, *"well, I'm going to go forward anyway,"* **you just failed the test to obey**. All you had to say, when I told you I wanted you to wait, was yes sir, I'll wait. That's all you had to say. If you had done that, I would have told you at that point, because you're willing to obey me, and wait, you don't have to wait. I would have told you; you can go forward now and start your ministry if you so desire. If you are not willing to obey me now, as your pastor, you will not obey me when you get out there pastoring on your own. I told him I can't be your pastor if you're not willing to obey me. I told the young man; you've been with me for twelve years. All I can do now is pray for you, that the eyes of your understanding is open, so you can see where you errored. So, he went and got his parents pastor at the Baptist Church to ordain him. Remember what I said earlier in chapter six, whoever ordained you, for whatever reason, that person is now your pastor, whether you want them to be or not, and whatever spirit rest upon them, also rest upon you. What I'm about to say, about what happened next, is a shame. This young man, ordination service was live stream, and I was watching it. This well-known pastor of the Baptist Church right here in Fayetteville North Carolina, got up and said this young man has been around here since he was three years old. Now that might be partly true, but it's not the whole truth. I think his parents were a member of that church, but he wasn't, and I think his parents join that church, when he was three years old. So that might be partly true but it's not the whole truth, because from 2006 until 2019 as an adult, this young man has been with me faithfully for twelve years. One day, I ran into this young man, and I invited him out to my church, and he came, and after he left that Sunday, never came back again. So, after a couple of months, I showed up at his place of business and invited him back out to church and he came and never left again for twelve years. Now, this Baptist church pastor stood up and said yes, he's been around here **with me** since he was three years old and it's time now to launch him out into his own ministry. When I heard that I said that's a shame, and that's just a flat out lie, to be coming from the mouth of the man of God, making it look like this young man has been with him for all this time, but in fact, has never sit under him as his spiritual leader, not one day. This young man has been with me for the last twelve years and you are lying to these people, and fabricating, a story to make it look like he's been with you, since he was three years old and is now time to launch him out into his own ministry. Remember the word **"Prevarication"** and what it means? *"the act of lying, a false or deliberate misstatement."* So, this young man's ministry is **starting out is being founded by his pastor, his spiritual father, built on a lie**.

Now, my spiritual son, which is my physical son, in my church decided, he, and his wife wanted to go and leave and help his good friend *(the young man)* start his church. I gave him leave, I said if that's what you want to do, I can't stop you, but you and your wife, are called to be here, under me. They left in the middle of our new church building project to go help this young man start his church. Now here is my test as his former pastor and his dad. Sometime later when they got ready to ordain my son as the assistant pastor in the new church that his friend had started, I was invited, did I go? You better believe I went, because weather he was right or wrong by leaving me, he is still my son and I will support him, because I love him. And that's where we miss it in ministry pastors, when it come to our spiritual sons and daughters, weather right or wrong, we should be there to support them, even if they done us wrong. Because that's what love does, it shows itself not being selfish, and it covers the multitude of faults. I believe that somewhere down the road, God would open a door, and you will be able to minister to them, and they will be able to see, how wrong they have been, and it was with, love and kindness how you drew them. Be a better you pastor, and church leaders, and you should always understand, that two wrongs doesn't make a right, and you are just two people that were wrong. Pastors, we are the spiritual parents of them, meaning as a parent, we are supposed to be the mature ones, and not the immature ones. Pastors, do you really know what the word **maturity** means? According to U.S. Army doctrine, *"**MATURITY** is the ability to place REASONING, ahead of EMOTIONS, and make decisions based upon REASONING, and NOT EMOTIONS."* Notice what this definition says, is the **ability**, that means you have to gain the knowledge to do this, <u>by changing YOUR way of thinking</u>. When you have gained the knowledge, you will always place **reasoning**, *(making a decision out of what you have thought about),* ahead of your feelings at that time. You now place that decision that you have **made out of thought**, ahead of your emotions, *(what you are feeling)*. Decisions made out of feelings, is never good. As a leader, you have to learn to put your feelings aside, and make your decisions based upon the knowledge that you have gained concerning that situation, and not emotions. Pastors, that means we are supposed to be better in our thinking, and our actions.

These are the things that I've learned while serving in the military, about maturity, and being a leader, and no one can ever take these things that I have learned away from me. You may retire, or you may even grow older, but you never lose, or forget the training, or what you've learned, because it has become a part of you.

Now, let me say this, because of my military service and having to move from place to place from time to time, before I became a pastor, I had the opportunity to serve under other pastors and to fellowship and also to be under for a time. God allowed me to see and experienced certain things that were not right in certain ministries. They would hold long drawn out services to make themselves look spiritual, and pastors, that's a big turn-off. Church service starts at 9:00 AM, and you don't get out until 3:00 PM, six hours later, that is crazy, and pastors, you wonder why people won't come back to your church. You hold service to long! You also have the nerve to say, we're not going to hinder the Spirit, or cut the Spirit off, but you look around each Sunday and there are less and less people at church, and you wonder why. Pastors, you have to learn how to disconnect from the Holy Spirit, and reconnect the next Sunday. Pastors and future leaders if you start service at a decent time, and end at a decent time, people will come back. You can't teach them what the Word of God says, if they are not there. One church we attended, the praise singers, song for three hours, it was like a concert, but it was just a regular church service. And after the singing was over, and the announcements, receiving an offering, and other preliminaries that were in between the singing, and the message, the pastor preached for another hour and a half. In another church we attended, they took up five different offerings. Why take up five different offering? If you're going to take up five offering, let me help you out pastors, this is what the person is going to do. If they're going to give fifty dollars in offering, they're going to come to church with five ten dollar bills, and they going to put ten dollars in each offering. Why waste all that time taking 45 minutes to take up five different offering, thinking you're going to get more, when you can take up one offering, and be done in 10 minutes, and that fifty dollars will be put in all at one time. Another church we attended, the pastor preached for three hours, and that's just to long. A persons tension span is only about 45 to 50 minutes before the mind starts to wonder off. In all these things, the Lord was teaching me something, and showing me things not to do when I become a pastor, and that we all must be tested before we are chosen.

Now, I know that most preaches are called, and chosen by God, but some preaches just went, they were never chosen or sent by God. Remember, I brought out earlier in this chapter in **Romans 10 :15** says, *"And how shall they preach, except they be sent... ."* Those pastors that went on their own have been tested time and time again, but they have never passed the test. That's why no matter what church they attend the pastor of that church would not license or ordain them, so they just went on their own. Now that I have been a pastor for twenty-seven years, I know when I am hearing from God to ordain someone or when to wait. God will show you that person's heart and why they are not ready yet, and what they are missing in their spiritual walk. We all must be tested. **Hebrews 4:15** says, *"...Jesus was in all points tempted,* (tested) *like as we are, yet without sin."* If Jesus was tested in every way, just as we are, but without sin, what do you think about us, we all must be tested before we can serve.

I am still talking to you about The Modern-Day Pharisees: The Uncovering, thirty-four years in ministry, what you can learn from my experience. The modern-day Pharisee, are all about themselves, and they do their deals in secret undercover, hidden, from the public eyes, so they think. Jesus said they stand on the street corners, praying long prayers to make themselves look spiritual. It still goes on today, but not on the street corners, but in the church building, long drawn-out prayers, and long services to make yourself look spiritual and holy. Jesus said you have your reward.

Now, don't get me wrong, pastors to be a better you, you must learn to spend quality time in prayer. What is prayer? Prayer is communication with your Heavenly Father. **Luke 18:1** says, *"that men ought always to pray, and not to faint."* Faint means to get weak and give up, and that means we should never give up on prayer. We are to pray always, and use prayer as a means of **communication, fellowship, praise, petition** and **intercession**. Don't give up prayer as a means of communicating with your Heavenly Father, because that's how He speaks to you. Prayer is what changes things; prayer shakes up the kingdom of darkness. Prayer is what break the chains of bondage off the people lives. Prayer is what gives us breakthrough, when we are believing God. If you have a problem with praying, you have to bring your flesh under control, and get your thinking right. Paul says, *"I keep my body under and bring it into subjection."* Paul took control of his flesh, his body, and you have to do the same, God is not going to do it for you, you have to do it.

You must learn to spend quality time in prayer in order to be a better you. What is my best time to pray? Let me tell you about myself as a pastor, I had a problem with spending quality time praying, and studying the word of God at night, because of sports. From 7 PM to 11 PM at night was sports time on TV. I would spend three to four hours sitting there in front of a TV watching sports. Now don't get me wrong, there's nothing wrong with watching sports, but everything is done in it's order, and in it's time. I didn't have a problem with getting up in the morning praying for an hour, because I was used to getting up every morning for twenty-two years at 4:00 AM, when I was in the military. My body was used to getting up early in the morning, we had a saying in the military, *"we do more before 9 AM than most people do all day,"* and that's because we got up so early. What I did, since I had a problem with watching sports for three to four hours every night doing sports season. I started praying at night when sports are on, and I did this to bring my flesh under control. I started having my prayer time, praying and studying when I didn't want to, because I wanted to watch sports. I did it because I wanted to get control of myself sitting there in front of the TV all that time watching sports. God will hear you if your prayer time is for an hour early in the morning, or for an hour late at night, or for an hour at noon day. It doesn't matter with God; prayer time is prayer time. Do you think God here you more because you get up at 5 o'clock in the morning and pray for an hour, and He hear me less, because I pray for an hour at 10 o'clock at night, or He hears someone that prays at noon day for an hour less. Do you think He here either of us anymore or less? Well, He doesn't, because prayer is prayer and God honors the prayer time. That's why I started praying at night, there's nothing wrong with praying early in the morning, if that's what you want to do, or there's nothing wrong with praying at night, if that's what you want to do, or there's nothing wrong with praying at noon day, if that's what you want to do also. I don't have a problem any longer sitting in front of the TV for hours on end, watching sports, or any show, or movies, because I don't do it any longer, I have delivered my flesh. I can't tell you the last time that I sit in front of the TV, and watch the entire basketball, football, or baseball game. Believe it or not, I didn't even watch the entire 2024 or 2025 Super Bowl game. Watching sports, it's no longer a priority for me. If you have a problem with sitting in front of the TV, watching sports, or any show, or movies then, maybe, just maybe, you need to change your prayer time, to when the sports are on, or whatever you're watching that has drawn you away from God. I believe everyone should start their day out with prayer. How long should I pray? I believe that's between you and God. I also believe that everyone should end their day with prayer. How long should I pray? I also believe that's between you and God. But I believe if the prayer time doesn't mean anything to you, it doesn't mean anything to God, because you did not put your all in all into it. I believe we all should spend at least an hour in prayer, whatever time you set for prayer time, morning, noonday, or night. **Matthew 26:36-41** says, *"Then cometh Jesus with them unto a place called Gethsemane, and saith unto the disciples, Sit ye here, while I go and pray yonder. And he took with him Peter and the two sons of Zebedee, and began to be sorrowful and very heavy. Then saith he unto them, My soul is exceeding sorrowful, even unto death: tarry ye here, and watch with me. And he went a little further, and fell on his face, and prayed, saying, O my Father, if it be possible, let this cup pass from me: nevertheless not as I will, but as thou wilt. And he cometh unto the disciples, and founded them asleep, and saith unto Peter, What, **could ye not watch with me one hour**? Watch and pray, that ye enter not into temptation: the spirit indeed is willing, but the flesh is weak."* I believe this is where we get praying for one hour from. Now, I know it says here, Jesus said, *"could you not watch with me one hour."* I know what you're saying to yourself, Jesus didn't say anything to them about praying when he went off a little further to pray, he just told them to watch. Why did He take Peter and the two sons of Zebedee with him in the first place? Not just to watch, but to watch, and pray, because when he came back and found them asleep, He said to them, "***watch and pray***, *that ye enter not into temptation."* So, yes, we should be praying for at least an hour. If you can't, you need to pray more so you can develop your prayer life to be able to pray for at least an hour. *"Watch and pray, that ye enter not into temptation: the spirit indeed is willing, but the flesh is weak."*

Let's talk about getting up early in the morning praying for an hour, where did we get that from? It says that Jesus in **Mark 1:35** *"And in the morning, rising up a great while before day, he went out, and departed into a solitary place, and there prayed."* I believe that's where we get, this getting up early in the morning, to pray comes from. I believe that there is a misunderstanding when the scripture says that Jesus rose early in the morning to pray. **The problem comes when you don't know what the early in the morning is**. What you probably don't know is this. Jesus's timetable was different from ours. Our next day or morning began one second after 12 midnight, but in Jesus's time, the Jewish timetable was different. His next day or morning began one second after 6 PM in the evening, which is referred to the next day or morning. So, when the scripture says that He arose very early in the morning, that early in the morning could have been 6:05 PM, 7 PM, 8:30 PM, 9 PM and so on, and so forth, until daylight. The scripture says, He, *"in the morning, rising up a great while before day."* A great while before day could mean anytime between one second after 6 PM and daylight, and not necessary what we think of when we say, very early in the morning, but it could be. But if you want to get up at 5 o'clock in the morning and pray, it's OK. Like I said earlier, before you start out for work, or venture out in your day, you should start it with prayer. How long should I pray? Let me answer that question this way. Why not pray for an hour. Can you give God one hour out of your day or night, fellowship in with Him.

All of us pastors were talking on zoom one Monday morning and we got to talking about prayer time, and my former pastors went around on zoom asking each pastor what your prayer time was. When they got to me, I said well, I used to get up early in the morning and pray, but I had a problem spending any kind of quality time at night praying and studying my word. I told them, I will get in front of the TV when the sports come on and I will sit there for the next two to three hours sometime four hours watching sports. When it was time to go to bed, I didn't spend any quality time praying. I would pray for ten to fifteen minutes maybe twenty minutes but that was it. I told them, God started dealing with me about getting my flesh under control. I was getting up in the morning praying, spending quality time praying, but God said that I needed to get my flesh under control when it came to sports. So, I made a decision that I would do the majority of my prayer time, or my praying would be when the sports come on. Sometimes I would pray not only an hour sometime two hours right there on my knees, getting my flesh under control and then when I get up in the mornings, I would pray anywhere from twenty to thirty minutes to start my day. When I get to my office, I put everything down before I do anything, I will go in the sanctuary turn some music on, and I will spend the next thirty minutes in prayer. Now I said that to my former pastor and his wife and they came down on me for that. Remember what this book is about, The Modern-Day Pharisees: The Uncovering, in this day and time, how it is their desire to impose their will on another, even against that person's will. They control the people, and everything had to be their way. My former pastor's wife said, *"no, you should spend most of your prayer time in the morning."* I said why, just because you want me to. God here me whether I'm praying in the morning or in the afternoon, late at night or early in the morning he hears me. I'm bringing my flesh under control by spending the majority of my prayer time where I had a problem with my flesh, and it works for me. Now, how are you going to tell me what I should be doing when it comes to my prayer time, when it works for me? I'm not wrong because I decided to pray at night, and you're not wrong because you decided to pray in the morning, and the next person is not wrong because they chose to pray at noon day. She tried her best to tell me and show me that I was wrong, and she was right. Here she goes, trying to impose her will, and her beliefs, and her desires on me. Now doesn't that sound like the modern-day Pharisee that I am talking about in this book. Only you know where you have shortcoming, when it comes to spending quality time with God. No one can tell you what's the best time for you to pray. Now if you're lazy and you have a problem with getting up early in the morning and praying, then your best time for prayer is to get your lazy self out of the bed, and be a better you, and spend at least an hour in prayer with the Lord. But if you are an early riser in the morning, but in the bed by 8 PM, then you might need to change up and start spending quality time praying for an hour at night, before you go to bed. If you are in the bed by 8 PM each night, then my question is, when do you spend any time studying the word of God? I know some people personally, by 8 PM, they are already in the bed. They get home about 6 PM, eat dinner, take a shower, spent ten to fifteen minutes in prayer, and the next thing you know 8 o'clock they're in the bed. I've tried calling them, and their spouse said, he's already in the bed. They don't push themselves to stay up to spend any kind of quality time in prayer or studying the word of God. There quality prayer time should be at night until they bring their flesh under control. The bed is calling you at 8 PM, and your flesh will do whatever you allow it to do, and it will answer the call if you allow it. It doesn't want to pray, you have to make it. What ever quality time you have set to spend with God is totally up to you, whether you get up early in the morning or late at night and pray, or at noon day that's your call. I say again, everybody should start the day out with prayer, and everybody should end the day before they go to bed with prayer, but you can't tell me, and I can't tell you, what's the best time for me, or you to pray. God hears us regardless of what time we choose to spend with him, 5 o'clock in the morning, noonday, or 10 o'clock at night, God still hears us. I encourage you leaders to be a better you in all that you do, and don't let your good be evil spoken of.

Pastors and church leaders, be a better you when it comes to people. There is no reason for you to yell or talk down to anyone, people make mistakes. They are not your people! They are God's people, and they should be treated with respect and dignity at all times no matter what they have done, or what mistake they may have made. Be a better you when you are the leader of others, you have to know when the smile, went to frown, or went to pat someone on the back, and say, it's ok, I know you'll do better next time. Leadership is all about building people up, and not tearing them down, but by influencing them in such a way that they are able to carry out the vision, or to accomplish the mission or task. As a former Non-Commission Officer (NCO) in the United States Army, the day that I was promoted to sergeant, and put on sergeant stripes, I was handed the Non-Commission Office's Creed on a card, and was told, be the example, and to lead by it. The very first two sentences in that creed is: ***"No one is more professional than I. and the second is; I am a Non-Commission Officer, a leader of soldiers."*** It's an individual thing, and you must be the example of a leader and always lead by example, so others will follow you. This creed became a part of me, and still is, to this day. The only thing changed now, is that ***I am a professional leader***

of God's people. Pastors, and church leaders, we are a leader of God's people, and words of encouragement will go along way, when talking to, or working with others, and not yelling, or talking down to them. When talking to others, a professional leader will always be able to maintain his or her professional conduct at all times. But on the other hand, a unprofessional leader will always lead with their mouth, saying the wrong things and using hurtful words. A unprofessional leader will always have a domineering leadership style, just like the Pharisees. And that's where the problem lies with selfish leaders, everything is always about you. When you yell or talk down to others, that's not being a professional, or good leader. **Proverbs 15:1-2** says, *"A soft answer turneth away wrath: But grievous words stir up anger. The tongue of the wise useth knowledge aright: But the mouth of fools poureth out foolishness."* Like I said, yelling or talking down to someone is not going to get them to change or do what you want them to do. **James 1:26** says, *"If any man among you seem to be religious, and bridle not his tongue, but deceiveth his own heart, this man's religion is vain."* If you can't control your tongue when talking to others, who is going to follow you as a leader? No one! Pastors, we are supposed to be the mature ones, and able to control our tongue. Do you remember the definition that I gave you for maturity earlier in this chapter? If you don't, go back, and look at the definition, because you can't operate in something you have no knowledge in. A good leader will always think before they open their mouth and let the wrong thing come out, because words are hurtful, and it will cause discouragement among those you are leading. **Jeremiah 31:3** says, *"...I have loved thee with an everlasting love: therefore with lovingkindness have I drawn thee."* When someone makes a mistake if you would take the time, to calm down and talk to them in a nice way and use loving and kind words, they will be quicker to receive from you, than yelling or talking down to them. Most people that work in your church are volunteers, they are not on salary, so there is nothing to keep them there. So why would you think that they would put up with you talking to them in this manner? They wouldn't! And they shouldn't! Pastors and future pastors, what will the Lord say about you, when you stand before Him at the judgment seat of Christ. Listen to what I am asking you! Not what you want Him to say about you, but what will He actually say about you, how you conducted yourself over His people? Pastors and future pastors, make a change now, and be a better you, because you did not become successful by yourself, there are a group of people that is associated with you and your ministry that make's you successful. No one ever became successful by themselves, somewhere you had help, directly, or indirectly along your way. So why would you treat, or talk to people in the manner that you are treating them. You wonder why when people leave your church, or your presence they never come back again. Can you blame them? I wouldn't come back either, or neither would you, if the shoe was on the other foot. It's all about how you talk to and treat people. How do you talk to and treat your children at home, especially your teenagers? Pastors and church leaders, your

children know you even when you think they don't. When your children are young you can tell them anything and they will believe it, because you are the parent. But when they grow-up and mature, and become young adults, you can't just tell them anything and expect them to believe it, because they won't. They are now at a point where they can think for themselves, and will now ponder that thing in their mine or question you about it. They see the hypocrisy in you and they will make their own decisions, even if it's the wrong one. So it is in ministry spiritually, you can tell a babe in Christ almost anything and they will believe it, because you are there Pastor, but as they grow and mature spiritually, you can't just tell them anything and expect them to believe it, because they won't. They will now question you about it, because in their spirit, they know what you said are done was not right. As of now, 2025, I have been in ministry for thirty-six years, and twenty-eight years pastoring, and I've seen young children's grow up in ministry with their parents, and when they become young adults, they can't wait to leave their parent's house. They see that their parents are not at home what they proclaim to be in church. **They see the hypocrisy, and that you are really not what you proclaim to be on Sunday**. They can't take it anymore, and that's why they leave your house prematurely. Pastors, be a better you, your first job is to be a better leader in your home, and to be the example that your children would want to follow.
Have you ever read in **Matthew 7:12** it says, *"Therefore all things whatsoever ye would that men should do to you, do ye even so to them... ."*

Pastors, what do you think Jesus is saying in this verse? He is saying, be the example that others would want to follow, and treat and talk to others the way that you would want to be treated and talk to yourself. Jesus talks about how to treat others in Matthew the 25th chapter, and He ends it with: *"...Verily I say unto you, Inasmuch as ye have done it unto one of the least of these my brethren, **ye have done it unto me.**"* Jesus is saying if you are treating others this way, you are treating Me this way. Be a better you and get rid of your hateful attitude, because no one wants to be around you, and no one cares to hear what you have to say because of that hateful spirit you carry with you. Even if you are teaching the word of God, no one cares to hear it from you. If you have a leader with this type of spirit, you can become a better you, by distancing yourself from people like this, because God has someone with a different spirit waiting for you. Be a better you, and believe God that He will lead you to a good leader who truly understands, and know what leadership is. A lot of pastors don't really know what leadership is, they think they do, they just make it up as they go along, and call it leadership. But you can't operate in something you have no knowledge in. According to current U.S. Army doctrine, *"**LEADERSHIP** is the process of influencing others to accomplish the mission by providing purpose, direction, and motivation."* To be a leader of people, you must be an influencer to them. Are you a good influencer by **leading by example**, and also providing **purpose**, **direction**, and **motivation**, to your people? Or, are you a bad influencer, by not leading by example, criticizing, putting your people down, and always finding fault in them, like my former pastor's wife did me, **according to the email she wrote in chapter eight?** Leadership is all about being a good example, and influencing people in such a way to get them to accomplish the mission or the vision, and not put them down. In being a better you, remember this, **<u>a good leader will always lead by example</u>**, and will never tell you to do what they're not doing themselves, **because that is called being a hypocrite**. Pastors and future leaders, we must be the example and all that we do, at all times. Leaders that do not lead by example, when challenged by others, there will always be a confrontation. Pastors, we must hold ourselves to a higher standard, and be the example that others would follow.

Let me end this chapter with this; be a better you, and keep yourself from sexual immorality, and seeking after strange flesh, and money. It says in **Jude 1:7** *"Even as Sodom and Gomorrha, and the cities about them in like manner, giving themselves over to fornication, and going after strange flesh, are set forth for an example, suffering the vengeance of eternal fire."* God warns us in the book of Jude about seeking after strange flesh, and committing sexual immorality, that there will be a day of reckoning, there will be a day of punishment. Pastors, you need to heed to this warning, and stop whatever it is that you're doing because God sees you, and He cannot bless mess. I believe I have been led by the Holy Spirit to talk to you about this because of what is going on with men and women that are standing in the pull-pit, in a pastoral position, in the church today. You are the modern-day Pharisee that I have been talking about throughout this book, hiding what you do from the public eyes, but exposed the people, and their sins. Now, I say men, and women, because there are some women that's pastoring, that are sleeping with the men in their church, and they have the nerve to be so bold to say, if men can do it so can we. And you're right, you have a free will to do whatever you want to do, but that does not make it right, and God is not pleased. You stand in the church, in the pull-pit, but yet hide your sins, men with men, women with women, men with women, women with men, seeking after strange flesh. It's an abomination in the sight of God! And no, God is not pleased. So I'm referring to you women as well as the men that are pastoring, and are running after strange flesh. Let's talk about strange flesh for a minute, and I'm talking to both male and female pastors, because there are some females that has done the same as some men. The opposite sex is not drawn to you, they are drawn to the anointing, that is upon you. That's what they drawn to, and when you run after this strange flesh, and commit sexual immorality, the anointing will leave you, and when the anointing leave you, so will he or she. They wasn't there for you, they was there because of the drawing of the anointing upon you. You now have caused your whole ministry to fall, because of sexual immorality, and there will be a public uncovering of your sins. You have fallen into the trap of the devil by seeking after strange flesh, and that's just what the devil wanted you to do. He makes strange flesh look so good, and enticing, to trick you and trap you. **James 1:14-15** says, *"Every man is tempted, when he is drawn away of **his own lust**, **and enticed**. Then when lust hath conceived, it bringeth forth sin: and sin, when it is finished, **bringeth forth death**.*" Look what God is saying here, running after this strange flesh, and being drawn away of your own lust, you will be enticed, meaning *it will be exciting, or desiring* to you, and you will commit sin, and that sin will bring death, or destruction to your ministry, and all that you do. If the devil can get you to fall as the pastor, the sheep will scatter, and that's what he wants. Pastors, the devil can make this strange flesh, and money looks so good, and tempting, but I encourage you to be strong in the Lord, and in the power of his might and stand against this temptation. I know I have been talking about strange flesh, but the same principle applies to the finances that come into your church, to do the right thing. You may not have a problem with seeking after strange flesh, but you may have a problem with embezzling, or miss using church funds. The devil can make all that money that come in, in your offering looks so good, and he will tempt you, to steal, when no one is looking, because you have no accountability. After my encounter in the early years of my ministry, which I talked about in chapter three, I learned to set boundaries for myself, as you should also. I never talk to, or council females in my office alone, I will always have my wife present with me. I never touch money that comes into my ministry, I have a finance committee that do the counting. When it comes to the money, I am only authorize to sign checks, and not count the finances that come in. You know why? It is too easy to steal when no one is looking, and the devil knows that, and he will tempt you to do wrong. Pastors every time you use church funds to take care of personal business, God sees you, and he is not pleased. **Luke 12:48** Jesus said, *"...For unto whomsoever much is given, of him shall be much required... ."* When you have been given much, you have a responsibility, and you are required to do the right thing with it, and not abuse it.

Pastors, I will end this chapter with this, there's nothing wrong with you receiving a salary from the church, when the church can afford to give you one. But if you have to get up and browbeat the people every Sunday to get them to give so you can get a paycheck, you're wrong. If your church cannot afford to pay you a salary at this time you need to go get a job! The bible says *"he that does not work shall not eat."* Be a better you, and take the pressure off the people trying to raise money every Sunday for your salary. If you are truly called of God to pastor He will sustain your ministry to include your salary. Until you can believe God for that, go get a job! If you will learn to do things God's way, the finances will come in for the mortgage or rent payment, even your salary, or whatever the need is. If you truly believe God for the financial need for your ministry, then stop browbeating the people to give. You must lead your ministry by example, you and your ministry must be a sower, because God **only** *"give seed to the sower,"* and that means individually, and collectively. **Galatians 6:7** says, *"...for whatsoever a man sow, that shall he also reap."* What is it that you or your ministry is sowing into? Are you really sowing, or are you faking it? Your congregation might not know what you're doing, but God knows and sees. I have no needs in my ministry, because we sow and my ministry is debt free. Pastors, stop letting the people have their way, just so they will stay at your church, you are wrong for letting them do that. The only reason you do that, is because you believe the more members you have the more finances that will come in, but that is not true. The ministry that God has placed me over, we now bring in more revenue every month with just a handful of members, then I did when I had 200 members. When it comes to the finances, it's not about the number of members you have, it's about the principle of sowing and reaping, giving and receiving. If God has done it for me, the principal is always the same, He will do it for you also if you can believe Him. When you allow people to come into your ministry and do things the way they want to do them, you are sowing the wrong things into your ministry. You are only hurting your ministry and yourself because God sees what you're doing, and He can't bless mess. Your musicians are playing in the night club on Friday and Saturday night and up playing in your ministry on Sunday morning and you let them do that so you will have musicians. Your praise singers are also singing and dancing in the night club on Friday and Saturday night and up singing for the Lord before the people on Sunday morning. They are straddle the fence, and Jesus said *"a man can't serve two masters, he* *would either love one or hate the other."* So which one they are really loving and which one they're really hating? Only God knows. Pastors, where is your integrity to allow this to go on in your ministry? But what are we talking about in this book, the modern-day Pharisee, the uncovering, how they do their deals in secret and stand before the public as though they're so spiritual and holy. God sees what you are allowing in your ministry pastors and He is not pleased, and that is why the finances is not coming in to your ministry the way it could. Pastors be a better you and make a change, because God can't bless a messy ministry. I'm a firm believer if you will make a change and be a person of integrity, and stand for what is right even a great personal cost, that means losing some members because of change, God will bless your ministry exceedingly, abundantly, above all that you can ask or think. I really believe that, you know why? Because God did it for me, and the bible says, *"there is no respect of persons with God,"* and that means He will do it for you also, when you learn to do it His way.

I believe the things that I have written in this book, will help you to be strong, and be a person of integrity, and do the right thing, at all time, at all cost, and in every situation, and it will make you a better person, and in return, a better leader. My prayer for you is that you learn from other people's mistakes, so that you don't fall into the same pitfalls and traps, when it comes to strange flesh, or money, but you can avoid them, and be a better you, and in return, you will be a better leader.

Chapter 11: Beware Of Man Pleasers

Pastors your ministry is not a fraternity or private social club, and it has absolutely no place for man pleasers. Let me tell you about how a man pleaser operates, and pastors you need to be aware of this. First, let me say a man pleaser is not really loyal to anyone, they are only in it for themselves. He or she may appear that they are, but they're not, because when they finish with you, getting what they desire, or a better opportunity come along, they are quick to move on to someone else. They lacked integrity, and lacked the ability to stand for what is right. A man pleaser is one that is all for himself or herself, a Judas, what can I get out of it? What is in it for me? They might not say these words out loud, but in their mind, and in their heart this is what they're thinking. A man pleaser is one that does not know how to stand or operate in faith. They talk a good game, they even teach a good game, but they don't know what it means, to stand in faith. He or she is one that would try their very best to get close to the head leader, so they can work their deals. To get in good with the head leader, they will have to cast doubt on the character of others. They will lie on others, and will fabricate and embellish stories, and put them down to be close to the head leader. They will make misleading statements to make themselves look good to the head leader. Their endgame is to be in position with the head leader so in the future when they need finances or any kind of support, they can get it. He or she has to find a way to discredit other leaders that is around the head leader. As the head leader, it is very important that you are aware of the character of everyone that is around you. **If Jesus had a Judas, you better believe you have one also.** A man pleaser is one that has or will sale or has sold their spiritual birthright, *(what God had planned for them)* **to get what they want NOW!** And they do it without even realizing what they have done, just as Esau did. **Genesis 25:31-34** says, *"And Jacob said, Sell me this day thy birthright. And Esau said, Behold, I am at the point to die: and what profit shall this birthright do to me? And Jacob said, Swear to me this day; and he sware unto him: and he sold his birthright unto Jacob. Then Jacob gave Esau bread and pottage of lentiles; and he did eat and drink, and rose up, and went his way: thus Esau despised his birthright."* Everything that was Jacobs, or that Jacob did should have been Esau's by birthright. Esau's name should have been changed to Israel and not Jacob's, but because of a unwillingness to wait, he gave it all the way by being a man pleaser. Unfortunately, that's what some leaders do today, they become man pleases to please their boss or the person in charge so that they can have favor to get what they want **NOW**. It makes you a very weak leader to have man pleases, or people pleasers, and yes people around you to praise you, and make you feel special or important. **Galatians 6:3** says, *"For if a man think himself to be something, when he is nothing, he deceiveth himself."* Pastors, the days of honoring yourself by having these type of people around you will soon come to an end, because Jesus Christ is the only one that should be honored with thanksgiving and praise. To do these things, or to allow these type of people around you, makes you a weak leader. A covenant is only as strong as it's leader, if you have a weak leader, you have a weak covenant, but if you have a strong leader, you have a strong covenant. **1 Corinthians 4:2** says, *"Moreover it is required in stewards, that a man be found faithful."* That means your head leader has to find everyone around him, or her, faithful. Until you have been found faithful, you're just a talker you have not been proven yet. Every man must be proven in your action, and not just your conversation, to see whether or not you are faithful. The man pleaser is all about him or herself, they will cast doubt on others loyalty to the head leader, so when something happened or is said, it is more than likely that the head leader would not believe them, but will believe the man pleaser. A man pleaser will always be needy, and not just in finances. **A man pleaser will always support the head leader, no matter what, even when the head leader is wrong.** <u>**They will always go along to get along**</u>. <u>**They will see it and not see it**</u>. <u>**They will hear it and not hear it**</u>. <u>**They will just do it, and not question it, even when they know that this is wrong**</u>. Even when the leader is wrong, or has made a bad decision in judgment, the man pleaser would say something like this, its ok pastor, everybody makes mistakes, **and to be honest with you I don't even care**. Pastors you might be saying why am I bringing this up? You need to be able to identify when you have a man pleaser in the midst of you. A man pleaser is already headed for a fall and don't even know it. Sooner or later, they will fall, and you don't want to drag your ministry down with them. I've been with my former pastor for thirty-four years, longer than any other pastor that is with him. I know what I have seen and learned about people, especially a man pleaser, over these thirty-four years of ministry. I've watched people come in and out of my former pastor's ministry, and when it come to the man pleaser when the rubber truly met the road they fail by the wayside, you couldn't depend on them to stand with you in faith. They **DON'T** know how to stand on their own two feet in faith, and their ministry is **NOT** successful. **James 2:17-20** says, *"Even so faith, if it hath not works, is dead, being alone. Yea, a man may say, Thou hast faith, and I have works: show me thy faith without thy works, and I will show thee my faith by my works. Thou believest that there is one God; thou doest well: the devils also believe, and tremble. But wilt thou know, O vain man, that faith without works is dead?"* **The man pleaser can't show you their works by their faith, because there is none**. Meaning they can't show you any extraordinary thing that has been manifested in their ministry or life by faith, because they have no action. **James 2:20** says, *"...faith without works is dead."* Richard Francis Weymouth translation of the New Testament says, *"faith without corresponding actions won't work for you."* Meaning, what you say and do must correspond with what God **HAS** said, and what you are believing in your heart. Faith is acting on what God has said. **Faith is an action word!** It requires something of you, it's more than just believing. Oh yes, it starts with believing, but it goes beyond just believing. Verse 19 says *"the devils also believe, and tremble."* In other words, James says, you don't have anything on the devils just by believing only. **You have to talk and act like it's already done**, and that's what makes it faith. If you're truly standing in faith, there will be some evidence in your life and ministry. But with the **man pleaser** there is no evidence, they get what they want from others because they want it **NOW**. They put on a façade, putting it on Facebook and social media, with flyers and video commercials, acting like their ministry is all of this or that, and very successful, when really is nothing. Some has even closed the doors and shut down the church, because they have no members. You have reaped what you have sown.

    The covenant that I was a part of, we had a man pleaser among us. We had fourteen pastors in the covenant, and thirteen of us pastors, knew that this one pastor was a man pleaser. He had all the characteristics of a man pleaser, he always wants to be around and talk with the pastor, always act like he was doing something for the pastor. He will always take credit for something someone else done, and when he is alone with the pastor, he is always casting doubt on the other leaders. The other leaders never said anything to his face about being a man pleaser, but I've spoken to him off-line, not in front of the other pastors. I told this individual stop being a man pleaser, and stop being a butt kisser to get what you want. Everyone sees what you're doing, and they don't really trust you, and all you are doing is hurting your own ministry, because you're going to reap what you are sowing. We knew he was a man pleaser by his actions. This person that I'm talking about, I invited him in time past to one of my men's conferences to be one of my guest speakers. Before the conference started, he looked around at all the men that was there, a full house, every seat filled, and he turned, and said to me, "pastor this is what I want. I want what you got." I said, what do you mean. He said, "just look around, man this is great! This is what I desire when I hold my men conference, but the people just won't come." After the conference was over, I had the opportunity to talk with him, and I told him, pastor you are coveting with I have, and expecting God to honor that for you, and He won't. **Hebrews 13:5** says, *"Let your conversation be **without covetousness**; and be content with such things as ye have... ."* You have to learn to be content where you at, and with what you have, and not be desiring what someone else have. You don't know what that person had to go through to get to or to have the things that they have. You have to learn to believe God for yourself by faith, that's what God honors, and He's a rewarder. The modern-day Pharisee is all about themselves, what they desire, and don't care how they get it. If your heart is not right, then God cannot allow you to even have the appearance that you are successful, because it sends the wrong message **to you**. It's saying to you, I can continue to do what I'm doing, even in my wrongness, and still be successful, and that's the wrong message. All fourteen of us pastors would come to my former pastor's church for the men's conference, and stay at the hotel. But the man pleaser who used to stay with us at the hotel, now all of a sudden, he has changed. He will come to the men's conference and stay at my former pastor's house, and I believe he stayed there so he can work his deals, by casting doubt against the other leaders. Pastors, you as the head leader should never allow your subordinates to stay at your house, and you should never stay at their's. Because there are certain things about you that your leaders, should never know, or see when it comes to you, and your actions. Pastors you are human, and you are subject to get too relaxed around them, and start saying and doing things that you shouldn't, and your leaders perspective of you will change. They might not ever say anything to you about what they have observed and heard from you, but they will always keep it in the back of their mind to use it whenever there's a need to. Pastors, you should never leave yourself open to this, you must learn to protect yourself at all times. Now, I will admit, when my former pastor first started coming to the state to visit my church in North Carolina, twice he stayed at my house, but after the second time, the Holy Spirit showed me and my wife, that this was an improper relationship, and he should never stay at my house again. So, from that day, he never stayed at my house again, he always stayed at the hotel when ever he would come to North Carolina to my church, until the day he dismissed me and my wife, from the covenant.

Now, let me tell you how this person *(the man pleaser)* came into my former pastor's life. I was used to this kind of behavior of high-ranking individuals in the military, so I was able to spot it right away. Also, he was bragging about it to me one day, and didn't even realize what he was saying to me. This is when my former pastor's ministry had grown to over 600 members, and at the Wednesday night midweek service a high-ranking military individual came in. He was not in his military uniform, but in a suit, clean as the board of health. He didn't come-in waving flags and blowing whistles or ringing bells and saying hey look at me, he set an observed for a while. He came faithfully every Sunday and faithfully every Wednesday night midweek service, just sitting and observing for about three months. Observing, how he can be a part of this, how he can get close to the pastor. He observed, who was in charge, who was the right-hand leader of the pastor, and who was second in charge. He developed his schemes, and ideas how he can have those people removed from their position so he can be in the pastor's right-hand leadership position. So, this is what he did to be first in charge next to the pastor. One day at lunchtime while in his military uniform since the pastor has never seen him in his uniform, and don't know his rank, he decided to show his high rank. The pastor being retired military, understands rank structure, and what different rank mean. He shows up at the church at lunchtime to see the pastor, but really, he showed up in his military uniform so the pastor could see his rank. He comes in and he say to the pastor, I didn't want anything, I was just free for lunch, and I thought I'll come by and see you. He says, since I'm here, I want to say this to you. I've been watching you pastor for about three months, and you do too much, you got too much on your plate. You need to focus more on teaching the people and let me take this load off of you, because you do too much. Now mind you the pastor already has a right-hand man, that takes the load off of his plate, that does everything for him. No one comes directly to the pastor for anything. Everyone goes through there a sign individual, and this individual that is the head leader, goes to the pastor, and no one else. The rank structure was already set in place, who reports to whom. But this man pleaser comes in and strokes the pastor's ego saying, pastor, you do too much, let my wife and I be the person in charge, and let everyone else answer to us, and we'll be the only ones that answered to you and your wife. That keeps people from knocking on your door interrupting you. Now remember all of this was already set in place, but the man pleaser sees something good, and he wants to be in charge next to the pastor. So, he undermines the other leader that was in charge so that the pastor would remove that person from that position and put him in that head, leadership position. The pastor now sees he's a high-ranking officer, and probably says to himself, I don't want this person to leave my ministry, that's a lot of tithes and offering that will come in. To make a long story short, my former pastor failed for the man pleaser and his scheme, and remove the other person, him, and his wife from their position, and put this person and his wife in the head leadership position. This decision caused animosity in the church, in the ranks of the leadership, saying how did this guy come in and just take over? He hasn't been here, but three months, and we get removed from our position, and he, and his wife get moved into this position. The only explanation my former pastor gave them is, will I'm the person in charge, and I believe you've been doing a good job, but I'm the pastor, and I want this person *(the man pleaser)* in this position. That was a bad decision for my former pastor, because about two years after that decision, he lost well over half of his membership. Like I said, earlier, a man pleaser is all about themselves, and he even fabricated things on my wife and I, so it would cast doubt on our loyalty to my former pastor. My wife and I were not trying to be the pastors right hand man; I've been with my former pastor, longer than anyone, and I'm fine right where I am. I'm not trying to be the pastors go to person, and I'm not trying to be the person that rub elbows with the pastor or hang out with the pastor, or stay at the pastors house. I know my place, and I never want to sow that type of seeds, because I don't want that foolishness going on in my ministry. Remember **Galatians 6:7** says, *"whatsoever a man soweth, that shall he also reap."* This person is now reaping what he sowed. He's now been in ministry, pastoring his own church, for over twenty years, but he has no members, and has nothing to show for over twenty years of ministry. No one ever stays at his church. Just before the pandemic in 2020, he told me, that his last four members left his church. No one ever stays, you know why, you're reaping what you sown. God sees your heart and he know your heart is not right and as a pastor, you have responsibility and accountability over the lives of others, and God cannot allow you to continue in ministry, or be successful. Oh yes, you might have a certain measure of success in ministry, but never on the level that God intended. This person and my former pastor would hold men's conferences, trying to make it look like they are very successful, because a few more people have shown up to the conference, but just because you got people at your conference, that doesn't mean you're successful. If there's only a few people that shows up at the conferences or at church service, my former pastor, and the man pleaser, would say things like this, this is all God wanted here, or you're the only ones that God wanted to be here. You say that because that's all showed up, but in fact is, the real reason why that's all that showed up, is because your heart is not right, and God could not allow anybody else to show up because it would appear as though your successful even in your sins. When those people leave the conference you're right back to where you were, no one is at your church, and that's a sad place to be. Until you own your wrongness, and repent, and ask God to forgive you, and go to those people that you have wrong, and ask them to forgive you, you'll never see the promises of God manifested in your ministry, in fact, you will begin to lose what you already have.

This person *(the man pleaser)* of his own admission, in 2019 said to me, "you and your wife for over twenty years has always come and supported everything me and my wife has ever done." That came from the mouth of this person that I am talking about, but what was sad about it is this, when my wife and I held our big event, our grand opening new church building dedication service, he and his wife did not come to support us. They call themselves supporting my former pastor, who didn't come because he wasn't the guest speaker, **so he thought**. I believe, my former pastor's wife told them, I wouldn't go and support them if I were you, because that is disrespectful to your pastor not to be the guest speaker. I know she probably said that to them, because she have said that to my wife and I many times, in time past about not going and supporting what they're doing, because they're not doing what is asked of them about tithing the tithes, and other things. My wife and I never listen to that, we always made our own decisions, and always went and supported everything that the other pastors have ever done. One thing I know about people that are easily deceived, they can't keep things to themselves, they can't hold water when you tell them something in secret, they will eventually slip up and tell it, even though they didn't mean to. So, this person decided that he wasn't coming either in support of my former pastor. Remember, I told you that a man pleaser is going to support the person in charge whether they right or wrong. I believed by faith that people would come out and support us, and they did, but I knew my former pastor and the other covenant pastor would not. Thank God our building dedication grand opening service was a great success, and we had almost a full house in attendance.

Pastors, I brought all this up to you to say this,

you need to know the characteristics of a man pleaser, because they will come into your ministry to work their deals and try to sell you on their schemes, and in return it will cause your whole ministry to fall. This is what the modern-day Pharisee does, they're all about themselves, and their desire is to force their will upon others. My former pastor membership is only a handful now compared to what he once had. Now that his membership has gone way down, he says, "it's not about how many members you have. If you're waiting on members, you've already missed the revelation of ministry." That's a copout! And that's just an excuse of having no members because of hidden sins. Pastors I beg the difference, and disagree with that statement. **The word <u>ministry</u> means, *"to teach"*.** Who are you teaching, if you don't have any members? Ministry is about reaching people with the gospel, so it's about having members, and it's about doing what God has commanded us to do, and that is to feed the sheep and feed the lamb. So ministry is about having members to feed them. It doesn't matter what you are doing in ministry, it always come down to reaching people with the gospel. There's no pastor that I know that doesn't want members. Those that have members want more members, because we called to feed the sheep and feed the lamb with two things, knowledge and understanding, and that's why it is about members, to feed them. If you don't have any members, do you really have a church, or are you really call to pastor? Everyone is not called to pastor, and maybe that's why you don't have any members. The term Pastor, means *"Minister or*

Shepherd, who has spiritual care over people." So who are you shepherding if you don't have any members? Some that are pastoring, maybe they were supposed to be just a leader in someone else's church, and maybe that's why you don't have any members. Now I will say this, is not about how many members you have, or counting members when God tells you to do something, when you have a God-given vision to do it. That God-given vision is not based on how many members you have, it is based on what God has shown you and have told you to do. Just as He told me to do, go with what I had, 27 faithful members and He built the building debt-free.

Well, that's the life of a man pleaser, many years in ministry, and you have nothing to show for your actions, you have reaped what you have sown. Leaders and future leaders, don't fall into this trap by being a man pleaser, or people pleaser, because there is nothing good at the end of the journey. **Proverbs 14:12** and **Proverbs 16:25** both say the same thing, *"There is a way that seemeth right unto a man, but the end thereof are the ways of death (or destruction)."* Pastors and future leaders, I challenge you to be the change, and stop being man pleasers, and stand up for what is right regardless of the consequences!

My prayer for you readers is that the information presented to you in this book has helped you to be better leaders and not fall into the same traps, and pitfalls of past leaders who lacked integrity, and had poor leadership skills. Learn from my mistakes, as well as others that has made mistakes, and let your integrity be your guide, and be the leader that God has called you to be, so He can make His present known through you to his people. **Pastors, and future leaders, you are not all that, you are human, and you are subject to error**. The people that I have talked about in this book, to include myself, you would probably say to yourself, I can't believe this, not them, not my pastors. Let me tell you about people, which you may already know, they are good at hiding what they do out in front of people, especially pastors, but behind closed doors, in secret, they are someone that you would wonder who they are. You would say, I can't believe that they would do such things, no not them. **Now, again of course, I'm not talking about all pastors, only those that I have been associated with over these thirty-four years in ministry, that I know firsthand what they do and have been doing.** I am only talking about a few, and I'm sure they have something negative to say about me also. But that's ok, because I talked about my self, "my dirt", in chapter three, but thank God, I made a change, and they can too. Pastors, It takes a real man, and a real leader, to admit and expose their own wrongness so that others can learn from your mistakes. But when you think that you are holier than others, you will never admit your wrongness. You will continue to lie, and hide what you have done, and try an take it to your grave, but remember the bible says, *"...be sure your sins will find you out."* There are a lot of pastors out there that have not made the change, to do what is right, by confessing their sins, and turning from them. God has given us all the space to repent, just as he did Jezebel, but if you refuse to do so, and bad things start happening to you, it's your own fault.

I pray that sharing this information with you in this book or audio file has help you to be a better person, to be a better leader in your church, and not only in your church, in your home, and on your job. I also pray that the information presented on the pages of this book, or audio file will help you to make a change in your life for the better. As I stated earlier in chapter three, if you have wronged others, I encourage you go to them, and apologize and ask them for forgiveness for the things that you have said, or done to them. Then go to God and ask Him to forgive you, because, you can't just bypass those people that you have wronged, and thank you can just go straight to God, and he will forgive you. Not so! The order that Jesus gave is in Matthew chapter five is, go to the person **first**, that you have wrong, and ask for forgiveness, to restore harmony, and peace. **Then go to God**, and ask Him for forgiveness. We find this in **Matthew 5:23-24,** it says, *"Therefore if thou bring thy gift to the altar, and there rememberest that thy brother hath ought against thee; Leave there thy gift before the altar, and go thy way;* **first be reconciled to thy brother***, and then come and offer thy gift."* **Reconciled** means *to restore; to win over; to make up; to bring into agreement or harmony.* Noticed **the first thing** Jesus said to do, go to your brother first *(those who you have wronged)*, and be reconciled, then come and offer your gift or petition. I believe if you will do this, God will open doors for you beyond your dreams, exceedingly, abundantly, above, all that you can ask or think, and I believe that you will see a great change in your ministry, and life.

God spoke a word a prophecy to me years ago by my former pastor's wife, saying, I have placed books in you, now, write them. So, out of obedience to what God has spoken, I am writing. When God tells you to do something, and you do it out of obedience, He will exalt it in due time. In writing this book I have had a joy unspeakable, and a piece, that surpasses all understanding. I believe I have written from a spiritual truth, that the Holy Spirit has inspired, and I hold nothing against anyone. I believe, I have accomplished the assignment that God has given me to write this book.

Remember this book is about The Modern-Day Pharisees: The Uncovering, thirty-four years in ministry, what you can learn from my experience in these three different churches that I was a member, and a leader in over these thirty-four years. This book was not written, out of anger, or to put anyone down, but to expose, and uncover what has been, and is still going on in churches today, and someone has to be man or woman enough to speak up, and uncover these things that has been hidden. Everything that is written here in, is to only help you leaders and future leaders to become better leaders, and to learn from others, so you don't have to repeat the cycle of mistakes.

I know the writing of this book might have sound

harsh, or with a strong fist, and you might not agree with what I said, or how I said it, but it was written this way intentionally. I wanted you to experience through the reading of this book, or audio file what we have experienced over the years in ministry, and it should NOT have been so. I have written it in the way it was said, or done, as I have experienced it. These things that I have written about in this book is to help you to be a better you and in return a better leader.

Those that are **guilty** of these things that I have written, will say this book is a lie. I'm sure they will even try and write books about me, and what I have written about in this book that refers to themselves as a lie, or liar. They will try their best to discredit this book. **They will definitely try to defend themselves when talking to others that has read this book, by saying, these things that has been said about me in this book is untrue**. First of all, no one knows it's you, but you, and God, and the devil, unless you open your mouth and tell on yourself, by trying to defend yourself, because I mentioned no one's name, or the name of anyone's church. Have you ever heard that old saying: *"that a hit dog will holler"*. Meaning, **I am guilty** of these things that has been written in this book, and that's why I'm speaking out against them, trying to defend myself and keep my character in tack. When people don't really know you, they will never believe that you would stoop so low, and do such things, because they think they know you. But when they here with their own ears what you have said or done, they will have a different view of you, because faith for anything comes by hearing. They might not ever say anything to you personally about it, but they will definitely think differently of you. **That's why I am thinking about releasing these recordings, because they will back up a lot of what I have written in this book.** I know what I have written in this book will be disputed, by the **guilty**, but that's ok, because the **guilty** always try to put the blame on someone else. God knows all things, and I have written what the Holy Spirit has instructed me to write. Remember this book is about what you can learn from my experience in thirty-four years of ministry. The whole purpose of this book is that you learn from my and other people's mistakes not to repeat them. I pray that the things presented to you in this book has taught you things to do, but also things not to do.

Pastors, people might not ever know anything about what you have done, or been doing, or even still doing, but remember, God sees, and knows all things, and He said, *"be sure you'll sins will find you out."*

Leaders and future leaders please do not treat your leaders in this fashion that you have read about from my experienced in this book. **Be a better you, and in return, you will be a better leader**. One thing I do know for sure is, if we don't learn from our past, history, or mistakes we are destined to repeat them.

Now let us hear the conclusion of the whole

matter of this book. So, I will like to leave you with this. The pharisee, and the modern-day pharisee crave only one thing, and that is absolute power. When you have no one to answer to, that absolute power will corrupt you absolutely, and it will corrupt your ministry. What you have forgotten is that the one key to your early success in ministry and your life was not absolute power, it was you always sought God. When you were small in ministry and yourself, you always trusted God, and God always came through for you, and you begin to thrive, and have good success. Everyone could clearly see that the hand of God was upon you and your ministry. Now that you have grown in ministry and statue, you stop seeking, and trusting God for your good success, you now start looking to your own strength and power to keep you there, as though you got there of your own accord. Pastors, because of absolute power, your success has become your downfall, and your ministry is just a shadow of what it once were. If your ministry, and life is not what it used to be, I encourage you to go back to the one key thing that got you there, and that is seeking God for your good success, and not absolute power. God is a faith God, and He is a God of integrity, and he will honor your integrity. **Proverbs 20:7** says, *"The just man walketh in his integrity: and his children are blessed after him."* Go back to what you know to be right, and be a person of integrity and stand for what you know to be right, even a great personal cost, and watch what God do in your ministry and life. **Proverbs 11:3** says, *"The integrity of the upright shall guide them: but the perverseness of the transgressors shall* *destroy them."* God is always looking for someone that walks in their integrity, and is full of faith that he can work through, will that be you? When you see wrongness, will you take a stand against it? **Will you stand for what is right even at great personal cost?** By doing GOOD, you will always do WELL, but absolute power will always corrupt absolutely. All it takes is one person to stand up, and speak up for what is right, for change to take place. *"If one can chase a thousand, and two can put ten thousand to flight,"* imagine what we all can do together when we stand up against wrongness. Remember what I told you in chapter four, that change and growth is never easy, and it may be slow, and there will always be naysayers and critics talking about what you can't do, but if you can believe that you can succeed you already have. All it takes is for one person to stand up for what is right for change to come, like I did in chapter two. You have two choices for change, either you can complain about it, and do nothing, or you can stand up and do something by speaking up. Your stand might be only a small victory, but that small victory will start a chain reaction that will lead to bigger changes in the future. Will you be the change, by standing up, and speaking up for what is right? Or will you continue to just go along to get along? Continue to see it and not see it? Continue to hear it and not hear it. Remember, change always begin with you, and not someone else.

I will end this book with a quote from Marcus Aurelius, *"The best revenge is to be unlike him who performed the injury."* I encourage you, don't be the person seeking after revenge against others that you feel has wronged you, because you are better than that! Let me tell you what I have learned over the years about revenge. If you are with your leader, or have moved on, <u>they are watching you</u>, and nothing torments the person that is against you more, **than watching you succeed <u>without them</u>**. Focus on peace, **and not payback**, because peace is the ultimate victory. Peace means, nothing they can say or do can break you and the one who can walk away calmly, always holds the real power. The bible tells us that your victory is already written, so walk in it and don't waste time or energy fighting what's beneath you. You owe it to yourself to never stay where you are no longer valued or respected, so move on and let them live with the chaos they created. Now don't get me wrong, forgive them for what they have done to you, because forgiveness frees you to move on and walk away with dignity. The strongest revenge is no revenge at all, do nothing, just remain silent. Remember, I told you in chapter eight, being silent isn't weakness, **<u>is strategy</u>**. Staying silent becomes your greatest power. Staying silent will confuse them, they don't know what to think, because your silence and you not engaging with them, ruins the games that they try to play. They will always wonder did they really get to you. The best revenge is to outgrow them, because once you rise above their level, you stop playing their games. When you outgrow your leader or others, it creates distance and distance creates resentment. They will resent you and put down all that you have, and all that you do, no matter how good it is, like my former pastor's wife did to me in chapter eight, according to the email she wrote. So don't give them the satisfaction of provoking you by engaging with them. A good leader knows that their authority speaks for itself, and you don't have to prove anything to anyone. So a good leader will never use revenge, because they know that silence and patience is their greatest weapon, and they just have to give it time. But on the other hand, a poor leader uses revenge as a weapon, but not understanding that revenge is weakness and it really shows how weak you are as a leader to abuse your power or authority just to get back at others that you feel has wronged you or don't agree with you. Just look at some of our church leaders and government officials today, how they abuse their power or authority just to get back at those that they feel has wrong them, or do not agree with their agenda. So I encourage you to let time do the work to heal you and use what happened to you as an opportunity for growth. Be a better leader, because through Jesus Christ you are. **Romans 12:14-21** says, *"Bless them which persecute you: bless, and curse not. Rejoice with them that do rejoice, and weep with them that weep. Be of the same mind one toward another. Mind not high things, but condescend to men of low estate. Be not wise in your own conceits. Recompense to no man evil for evil. Provide things honest in the sight of all men. If it be possible, as much as lieth in you, live peaceably with all men. Dearly beloved, avenge not yourselves, but rather give place unto wrath: for it is written,* **<u>Vengeance is mine; I will repay, saith the Lord</u>**. *Therefore if thine enemy hunger, feed him;*

if he thirst, give him drink: for in so doing thou shalt heap coals of fire on his head. Be not overcome of evil, but overcome evil with good." In other words, be kind to others no matter how they have treated you. Be a better you, don't seek revenge against others that you felt that has done you wrong, because this is what the modern-day Pharisee do. Remember what I brought out earlier in this book, **wise men said: "Don't seek revenge. The rotten fruits will fall by themselves."** See, you don't have to do anything to them, because they have done it to themselves. As I stated in chapter one, I believe God gives every person the space to repent, but your pride won't let you. You have every opportunity to repent, and make things right against those you have wronged, but you refuse to do so, because you have lost the fear of God. **Hebrews 10:30-31** says, *"...The Lord shall judge his people*. **It is a fearful thing to fall into the hands of the living God."** This word **fearful** truly means, you as a leader should be afraid of what awaits you at the judgment seat of Christ because of what you have been doing, or not doing as a leader. Don't seek to get back at others, turn them over to God. Absolute power will always lead you down the road of revenge against others, who you feel have wronged you. Don't go down that road, because there is no peace at the end of your journey.

If I decide to release the recordings that I talked about earlier in this book, they will be posted on my website. They will back up a lot of what I have talked about in this book, **if I decide to release them**.

My ONLY intent of releasing them, **if I decide to do so**, will only be so you can hear for yourself how we all have been talked to, and treated over the years by my former pastors, and others. My prayer is, as you listen to them, you learn from these recordings that you as a leader, doesn't talk to, or treat your people this way.

Now, I talked about recording someone's conversation without their permission in chapter eight, so I will repeat it again so you will know. First of all, laws vary from state to state, so make sure you look up the law for your state before recording someone's conversation, as I did. In the state of North Carolina, where I live, you **DON'T** have to inform the person that you are recording them. North Carolina is considered a **one party**, or a **single party** state, meaning you don't have to inform the person or persons, that you are recording. I wish you readers could hear the recording that I made of the conversation of my former pastor's wife, when they dismissed us from the ministry, she was so angry, she just went on continuing to tell us off! The problem I see with most people when you inform them that you're going to record them, they are so arrogant, or mad, they will say *I don't care what you do,* because they think you're really not going to record them. With technology today, all it takes is an app on your phone, and press it to start recording, but arrogant, mad, and prideful people don't think you will. I want you to know, I have no intent of releasing these recordings at this time, that is not my purpose in recording, or writing this book. **These**

recordings is only evidence, and proof for myself about what has been going on for years in ministry.

Continue to check back, from time to time on my website for the posting of the recordings, if I decide to release them. **Visit my website at: www.jwocnc.org.**

Philippians 1:6 says, *"being confident of this very thing, that he which hath begun a good work in you will perform it until the day of Jesus Christ."*

Luke 12:2 & 3 Jesus says, *"For there is nothing covered, that shall **NOT** be revealed; neither hid, that shall **NOT** be known. Therefore whatsoever ye have spoken in darkness **shall be heard in the light**; and that which ye have spoken in the ear in closets **shall be proclaimed upon the housetops."***

The International Bible says, in **Proverbs 11:21,** *"Be sure of this: The wicked will not go unpunished, but those who are righteous will go free."*

Revelation 2:29 says, *"He that hath an ear, let him hear what the Spirit saith unto the churches."* Thank you for reading or listening.

May God continue to bless you and keep you.

Other books published by this author:

"Breaking Traditions"

www.ingramcontent.com/pod-product-compliance
Lightning Source LLC
Chambersburg PA
CBHW032103090426
42743CB00007B/217